W9-BVD-737

PINTER: THE PLAYER'S PLAYWRIGHT

The author and publishers are most grateful to Harold Pinter for taking the trouble to provide certain information concerning his life in repertory companies. It should be stressed, however, that the conclusions drawn are entirely the author's own.

PINTER

THE PLAYER'S PLAYWRIGHT

David T. Thompson

Schocken Books • New York

First American edition published by Schocken Books 1985
10 9 8 7 6 5 4 2 1   85 86 87 88
Copyright © David T. Thompson 1985
Published by agreement with The Macmillan Press Ltd, London and Basingstoke

Library of Congress Cataloging in Publication Data
Thompson, David T.
Pinter, the player's playwright.
Bibliography: p.
1. Pinter, Harold, 1930-   —Knowledge—Performing
arts.   2. Pinter, Harold, 1930-   —Biography—
Careers.   3. Dramatists, English—20th century—
Biography.   4. Actors—England—Biography.   I. Title.
PR6066. I53Z84   1985   822'.914   84-23464

Printed in Great Britain
ISBN 0-8052-3964-2

To Leslie and Pam

Contents

Acknowledgements

I am deeply indebted to Mr Harold Pinter. His kindness and helpfulness I consider a special privilege, and I should like here to express my sincere gratitude for the information he provided and which he seemed to take a delight in offering me.

I wish to thank Leslie Smith for his invaluable help in structuring the work in its initial form as a thesis. Any coherence to be found in the style or argument is largely the result of Leslie's conscientious and disciplined work as my tutor at the North London Polytechnic.

My thanks are also extended to Dr Katharine Worth, Professor Peter Davison, Mr Barry Foster, Mr Guy Vaesen and Mr N. F. Simpson for the information they provided and for their interest and encouragement.

I am also grateful for the assistance I received from the staffs of the British Newspaper Library at Colindale; the British Drama League, Fitzroy Square; the North London Polytechnic; and the Westminster Reference Library. My special thanks go to Sue Maddox for painstakingly deciphering manuscripts in order to produce the original draft, and to my wife, Pam, who has acted for the past five years as a most tolerant and exceedingly charitable personal manager.

Finally, I wish to express my debt of gratitude to Mr Dennis Griffiths, who not only introduced me to Harold Pinter's work, *The Birthday Party* in particular, but also gave me a better appreciation of what might happen on a stage.

1 The Player's Playwright

Harold Pinter, talking about his work and career with Richard Findlater, acknowledged a connection between his work as an actor and his plays: 'Yes my experience as an actor has influenced my plays – it must have – though it's impossible for me to put my finger on it exactly.'[1] Only a couple of years after he had ceased acting on any regular basis he thus declared a relation between his own acting-experience and his plays. At the same time, however, he could not precisely analyse the connection. That inability may be accounted for in various ways: first, at the time of writing he had had little time to reflect on any debt he might owe to his recently finished full-time acting-career; secondly, he had performed in so many different plays, mostly quickly rehearsed, performed and forgotten in the hectic world of repertory theatre; thirdly, there is the natural reluctance of any creative artist to conceptualise or pin down the sources of his work. The second reason might be considered the most relevant when one considers the number and variety of plays Harold Pinter acted in throughout the 1950s: he began in the main with Shakespearian drama and Greek tragedies, and then performed in a host of contemporary West End successes such as formed the diet of the provincial repertory companies of which he was a member – a diet of thrillers, light comedies, romances and farces.

If the playwright himself cannot put his finger on it exactly, the task facing anyone trying to do it for him is surely a daunting one. Pinter's own distinctively individual plays seem a far cry from the Shakespeare and Sophocles, the Agatha Christie and J. B. Priestley that had formed the staple material of his acting-career. Just how distant a cry is perhaps suggested by the early, almost universal critical and popular dismissal of *The Birthday Party*'s mysterious ambiguities – '*The Birthday Party* . . . went off in a week. Most of the critics massacred it. No one came'[2] – and the later hostile provincial reception given to *The Homecoming* with its strange, apparently undermotivated acts of sex and violence. John Normington, the actor, remembers:

1

The first night in Brighton I shall never forget. . . . The audience heckled and booed. While we were saying lines they actually shouted 'What nonsense! Oh what rubbish!' They stormed out and there was no applause at all. . . . We knew it was going to be tricky in Brighton. Peter Hall came round and said, 'I had a look at the house and don't expect a lot from them.' They'd come in their tiaras and they only want Flora Robson. [3]

But the connection between Pinter's early repertory experience and his own work is felt not only by the playwright, but also by actors who have appeared in his plays:

I'm sure his actor's instinct plays a large part in the making of his plays.

Everything in the play *The Homecoming* was tried and tested before we got it: everything was utterly speakable. There is not a single line which had to be cut in order to make it speakable. This is an actor's instinct. Ordinarily, you have to cut many things which will not fall off the tongue. In Pinter the words really do come off the tongue and teeth beautifully. [4]

The connection is also made by some critics who have wished to denigrate his work and have chosen this line of attack to do so. The plays have been seen as vehicles for mere self-indulgence – on Pinter's part and on the part of his actors. For Bernard Levin Pinter has constantly seemed to be merely 'imitating his own style, asking himself what Pinter would do now, and then doing it'. Clive James has dismissed *No Man's Land* as typical of the playwright, 'a con' which 'consisted entirely of its own technique'. [5] Earlier, Nigel Dennis reduced a Pinter play to the level of a drama-school improvisation exercise and yet quite clearly saw the importance of the actor in Pinter's plays. In reviewing critical works by Martin Esslin and J. R. Hollis, Dennis made a challenging statement that the plays were all technique and no substance:

I would like to suggest that the proof of the pudding is in the acting. . . . This appeal to actors is due, I think, to the fact that Pinter himself was a professional actor before he took to play-writing and is still acting when he supposes himself to be writing: this is the nature of the 'intuition' of which Mr Esslin speaks so warmly. Mr Esslin and Mr Hollis are convinced that his intuition is guided by some deep understanding of human nature; in fact, the understanding is of nothing but of what an actor can do. Any ideas that are present in Pinter plays are merely secondhand oddments inherited from more thoughtful playwrights: the originality of all the plays lies in the very peculiar scope they offer to the actors in them.[6]

Quite clearly these critics have lost patience with the enigmas, the difficulties and the uncertainties in Harold Pinter's work. Perhaps Dennis's attack is also fuelled by his irritation with the more presumptuous and pretentious interpretations offered by critics of the plays. Critics indeed have filled in the gaps, pauses and unexplained motivations in Pinter's plays with all manner of fanciful philosophical and psychological interpretations. This is a playwright, Dennis surely feels, who must be brought down to earth. Yet, ironically, Pinter would probably agree with Dennis's impatience with some of the more pretentious approaches to his work. He has referred to some of the psychiatric conjectures about *The Homecoming* as rubbish and has added, 'I've never started a play from any kind of abstract idea or theory and never envisaged my characters as messengers of death, doom, heaven, or the Milky Way.'[7]

Dennis's provocative review with its insistence that Pinter is indeed a player's playwright but in a pejorative sense provides, then, a useful starting-point for the present analysis. I aim to explore the connections between actor and playwright acknowledged by Pinter, and to refute the line of attack followed by James, Levin and Dennis.

The study will examine Pinter's working-conditions as a young actor, the plays he performed in and his recognition of what an actor is and what he can do in the theatre, and consider the plays in the light of these matters. In the course of this examination it will be suggested that the unique quality of much of Pinter's work is appreciably produced by an amalgam of different kinds of theatre within his own experience: the classical drama, the provincial repertory's diet of West End derivatives of the 'well-made play', and, supplementing this, an interest in forms of popular theatre, present in the Elizabethan repertory, but represented also in the seaside provincial towns where Pinter mainly acted by music-hall and variety performers such as Frankie Howerd, Arthur Askey and Tommy Trinder, and by such radio and television comedies as *Hancock's Half Hour* and *Take it from Here*. In the more striking language of Peter Brook, these three categories may be designated 'Holy Theatre', 'Deadly Theatre' and 'Rough Theatre'; and it is the last-named, significantly, that Brook values most: 'Every attempt to revitalise the theatre has gone back to popular theatre.'[8] Pinter's work as an actor involved him in all three: the ritualistic, ceremonial tragedies of the Greeks, the second-hand quick run-throughs of the repertory theatre, and the rougher experiences of a travelling popular theatre in Ireland, playing Shakespeare – the dramatist in whom, as Brook asserts, Rough Theatre, with its audience involvement and popular appeal, and Holy Theatre come together.

Harold Pinter's first experience as an actor was at school. He attended Hackney Downs Grammar School in East London in the 1940s and took the male leads in *Macbeth* and *Romeo and Juliet*. It is worth mentioning that as a schoolboy he was taken to see Donald Wolfit's *Macbeth* and *Lear*. He recalls his English master taking 'a few of us to see Wolfit, and that left a great impression. *Lear* particularly, which I saw six times. I couldn't stop seeing it.'[9]

Between autumn 1948 and summer the following year Pinter spent an unsettled time at the Royal Academy of Dramatic Arts, where he is on record as having played Pistol in *The Merry Wives of Windsor* and Edward Moulton in *The Barretts of Wimpole Street*, 'both of which performances were favourably remarked'.[10] Pinter himself, however, has since been prouder of the acting-talent he displayed in faking a nervous breakdown in order to leave RADA, yet retain the grant: 'One trains oneself to become extremely white in the face. Then you have to speak in a very low voice, hardly heard, and walk very slowly, and be on the verge of tears.'[11]

This conscious adopting of a role to get out of an uncomfortable situation had come in useful to Pinter earlier in his life. Whereas at RADA he was a 'very unsophisticated young man . . . full of contempt for so many things in those days'[12] who sought escape from a society that seemed too dauntingly sophisticated, previously he had had to act his way out of potentially violent situations:

Everyone encounters violence in some way or other. It so happens I did encounter it in quite an extreme form after the war, in the East End, when the Fascists were coming back to life in England. I got into fights down there. If you looked remotely like a Jew you might be in trouble. Also, I went to a Jewish club, by an old railway arch, and there were quite a lot of people often waiting with broken milk bottles in a particular alley we used to walk through. There were one or two ways of getting out of it – one was a purely physical way, of course, but you couldn't do anything about the milk bottles – *we* didn't have any milk bottles. The best way was to talk to them, you know, sort of 'Are you all right?' 'Yes, I'm all right.' 'Well that's all right then, isn't it?' And all the time keep walking towards the lights of the main road.[13]

After a year he tried again at drama school, this time the Central School of Speech and Drama, and stayed for a year only.

Pinter has not acknowledged much of a debt to his drama schools:

I was very unhappy at . . . RADA. I was much too young and really hated it. Everyone seemed to be so sophisticated and know exactly where they were.

Q. Were the Drama Schools of any use to you as a playwright?
A. None whatsoever. It was just living.

I had a certain ability of a limited kind as an actor, and I couldn't see any other way of earning a living.[14]

Closely following this stay at the Central came some minor work in radio dramas and documentaries and in a pantomime before Harold Pinter truly began his career as a stage actor. That career started not in London but in provincial Ireland.

2 Apprentice to Two Masters

During late 1950, 1951 and 1952 Pinter experienced, in his own phrase, 'a golden age',[1] touring Ireland with one of the last of the great actor–managers, Anew McMaster. McMaster had been an itinerant actor–manager from 1925 onwards, taking his company around Ireland and across the world in a repertoire of classical and Shakespearian plays. The roles which made his reputation were Hamlet, Macbeth, Coriolanus, Petruchio, Richard III, Shylock and, above all, Othello. Rarely playing outside his company, unconnected with films and television, he explained his nomadic existence with the comment, 'I suppose I'm a wanderer and I like playing in the theatre. It makes no difference to me if I'm on Broadway or in the smallest village hall in Ireland. The only thing that matters is that I am playing.'[2]

Pinter's first contact with McMaster, then fifty-six, was through an advertisement in *The Stage* for actors to play Shakespearian roles on a tour of Ireland. Pinter sent a photograph, was interviewed by McMaster in a flat near Willesden Junction, and was offered £6 a week and the parts of Horatio, Bassanio and Cassio. In the event Pinter played many more roles than these three and the experience gained in the rough conditions of a touring repertory company must have provided a baptism of fire for the young actor. The company toured the towns and villages of Ireland from Limerick and Dundalk to Ennis, Bandon and Cloughjordan, and Pinter played Iago and Cassio in *Othello*, Horatio in *Hamlet*, Bassanio in *The Merchant of Venice*, Macduff in *Macbeth*, Edmund and Edgar in *King Lear*, Hortensio in *The Taming of the Shrew* and Charles the Wrestler in *As You Like It*; in addition he played Creon in *Oedipus* by Sophocles, and three Wilde roles – John Worthing in *The Importance of Being Earnest*, Lord Windermere in *Lady Windermere's Fan* and Sir Robert Chiltern in *An Ideal Husband*.[3]

Years later, in 1968, Pinter was to write a memoir of his years with McMaster, as a retrospective tribute to the actor–manager, who had died in Dublin in 1962. 1968 was the year in which Pinter was beginning to explore dramatically 'time remembered', in the writing of *Landscape* and *Silence*. It was perhaps natural, then, that he should look back with peculiar sharpness of vision and delight to his first days as a professional actor, and in particular to the man who set him on the road to eventual success in the world of theatre. Memory in Pinter's plays may be a treacherous and deceptive thing, but the detail, clarity and confident narrative technique in this autobiographical memoir of his days on the road in Ireland shows no ambiguity. Pinter here describes the basic, Bohemian and nomadic qualities of his days touring with 'Mac' McMaster:

> The people came down to see him. Mac travelled by car, and sometimes some of us did too. But other times we went on the lorry with the flats and props, and going into Bandon or Cloughjordan would find the town empty, asleep, men sitting upright in dark bars, cowpads, mud, smell of peat, wood, old clothes. We'd find digs; wash basin and jug, tea, black pudding, and off to the hall, set up a stage on trestle tables, a few rostrum [*sic*], a few drapes, costumes out of the hampers, set up shop, and at night play, not always but mostly, to a packed house . . . . [4]

Pinter also responded with great warmth and affection to the character of Anew McMaster himself, in particular his larger-than-life personality and his idiosyncratic manner of speaking. Pinter attempts to sum up McMaster's many-sided personality as belonging to a man who 'was evasive, proud, affectionate, mischievous, shrewd, merry, cynical, sad, and could be callous'. [5] McMaster's manner of speaking is directly represented on several occasions in Pinter's memoir, and, given Pinter's acute interest in and remembrance of those happy years, his reproduction of McMaster's style of speaking is doubtless substantially accurate. Here follows an example of the staccato, lively, nervous yet confident vein of McMaster:

> If the clergy call say I am studying King Lear and am not to be disturbed. . . . I can play the part. It's the lines I can't learn. That's the problem. The part I can do. I think. What do you think? Do you think I can do it? I wonder if I'm wise to want to do it, or unwise? But I will do it. I'll do it next season. Don't forget I was acclaimed for my performance in 'Paddy The Next Best Thing'. [6]

It is axiomatic that Pinter has shown in his plays an ability to capture the repetitions, non-sequiturs and stop-and-start rhythms of everyday speech; it is more than arguable that Anew McMaster was one of the more inspirational stimuli of this ability. In his memoir of McMaster, Pinter has pictured a harassed but still authoritative patriarchal figure, a theatrical father figure responsible for his company–children. At the very beginning of Pinter's homage to his first theatrical employer we are presented with a 'grand old man' of the theatre, his authority now perhaps a little on the wane, a little under threat, but propped up by memories of a past glory:

> I've been the toast of twelve continents and eight hemispheres! Mac said from his hotel bed. I'll see none of my admirers before noon. Marjorie where are my teeth? His teeth were brought to him. None before noon, he said, and looked out of the window. [7]

As a leading actor of the 'old school', McMaster could be fiercely concerned about the primacy of his position on stage – no member of his company could upstage him without incurring vituperative recriminations afterwards:

> Those two? It must be like two skeletons copulating on a bed of corrugated iron. (The actor and actress Mac was talking about were very thin). He undercuts me, he said, he keeps coming in under me. I'm the one who should come under. I'm playing Hamlet. But how can I play Hamlet if he keeps coming under me all the time? The more under I go the more under he goes. Nobody in the audience can hear a word. The bugger wants to play Hamlet himself, that's what it is. But he bloody well won't while I'm alive. [8]

It is easy to understand the existence of fierce in-fighting and bitchiness in a theatrical company that has been long on the road together in close and cramped conditions. Pinter also refers to McMaster as 'a very great piss-taker' [9] and illustrates his point by remembering a story against himself:

> In the trial scene in *The Merchant of Venice* one night I said to him (as Bassanio) instead of 'For thy three thousand ducats here is six', quite involuntarily, 'For thy three thousand *buckets* here is six.' He replied quietly and with emphasis: 'If every *bucket* in six thousand

buckets were in six parts, and every part a *bucket* I would not draw them – I would have my bond.' I could not continue. . . . Mac stood, remorseless, grave, like an eagle, waiting for my reply.[10]

Pinter's plays are full of characters striving to retain a sense of authority, or figures struggling to maintain a pride in self. Max in *The Homecoming*, Goldberg and Stanley Webber in *The Birthday Party*, Hirst in *No Man's Land* and Roote in *The Hothouse* spring readily to mind. Something of McMaster in his role as vulnerable father figure to his company is caught by Pinter's portrayal of Max, the titular head of his North London household, in *The Homecoming*. In Max we also see the waning authority of the father figure compensated for by boastful recollections of the past.

Many times I was offered the job – you know, a proper post, by the Duke of ... I forget his name ... one of the Dukes.   (p. 26)

I remember one year I entered into negotiations with a top-class group of butchers with continental connections. I was going into association with them.   (p. 62)

With perhaps more bitterness than McMaster, Max too indulged in bitchy attacks on his brother and sons whenever he felt his position of authority threatened:

A crippled family, three bastard sons, a slutbitch of a wife – don't talk to me about the pain of childbirth – I suffered the pain . . . and here I've got a lazy idle bugger of a brother won't even get to work on time. The best chauffeur in the world. All his life he's sat in the front seat giving lovely hand-signals. You call that work? This man doesn't know his gear-box from his arse!   (p. 63)

Pinter's plays also involve many examples of linguistic oneup-manship, the manipulation of language for purposes of mockery, point-scoring, achieving tactical victory in some battle over territory or relationships. 'Taking the mick' or 'piss-taking' – something that Pinter responded to with delight in McMaster – is put to serious dramatic use in many of Pinter's plays: Mick taunting Davies in *The Caretaker*; Lennie provoking Teddy in *The Homecoming*; Briggs and Foster putting down 'friend' Spooner in *No Man's Land*.

And in this connection we can see a conscious or unconscious echo of McMaster's insistent playing with the word 'bucket' in Davies's own attempt to keep his end up as a skivvy in a workers' café:

> Comes up to me, parks a bucket of rubbish at me tells me to take it out the back. It's not my job to take out the bucket! They got a boy there for taking out the bucket. I wasn't engaged to take out buckets. My job's cleaning the floor, clearing up the tables . . . nothing to do with taking out buckets! . . . Even if I was supposed to take out the bucket, who was this git to come up and give me orders? . . . I told him what to do with his bucket. (pp. 18–19)

Two other aspects of McMaster, as recalled by Pinter, seem of relevance to the latter's plays: McMaster's delight in role-playing and his vivid, loquacious monologues. On the first point, all actors change roles as a fundamental part of their professional experience; some, like McMaster, could not stop off stage. Pinter remembers his miming Marguerite, Faust and Mephistopheles to a record of *Faust* in a 'long golden wig' following performances of *Othello*; Pinter also recalls McMaster telling a story against himself, about being introduced by an Australian mayor as 'an actor who has given tremendous pleasure to people all over the world, to worldwide acclaim ... Andrew MacPherson!'[11] Pinter puts to his own serious dramatic use this 'theatrical' need for role-playing, for adopting a variety of different names, for it answers to his sense of the impossibility of knowing our fellow men, or even our own identity, in an exact and final way. Thus, Pinter's characters from Stanley Webber in *The Birthday Party* to Hirst in *No Man's Land* adopt poses or different personae, and various characters, such as Goldberg in *The Birthday Party* and Davies in *The Caretaker*, assume different names. (Actors, too, often adopt stage names: Pinter later became known professionally as David Baron.) With reference to the second point, the use of expansive monologue, echoes of McMaster's speech patterns and narrative flow can occasionally be picked up in moments in *The Birthday Party* when Goldberg holds the floor. Here is Pinter's reminiscence of McMaster in full expansive mood, with speech embellished by humorous asides, a punch-line, and a 'throw-away' anti-climax to boot:

> Look out the window at this town. What a stinking diseased abandoned Godforgotten bog. What am I playing tonight,

Marjorie? . . . But you see one thing the Irish peasantry really appreciate is style, grace and wit. You have a lovely company, someone said to me the other day, a lovely company, all the boys is like girls. Joe, are the posters up? Will we pack out? I was just driving into this town and I had to brake at a dung heap. A cow looked in through the window. No autographs today, I said. Let's have a drop of whisky for Jesus' sake.[12]

Now, Goldberg in full flow – with Lulu on his lap – is story-telling in the party scene in *The Birthday Party*:

I had a wife. What a wife. Listen to this. Friday of an afternoon, I'd take myself for a little constitutional, down over the park. Eh, do me a favour, just sit on the table a minute, will you? . . . A little constitutional. I'd say hullo to the little boys, the little girls – I never made distinctions – and then back I'd go, back to my bungalow with the flat roof. 'Simey' my wife used to shout, 'quick before it gets cold!' and there on the table what would I see? The nicest piece of rollmop and pickled cucumber you could wish to find on a plate.   (p. 69)

Here is the same relish for narration, the same tendency to digress to more practical matters, the humorous anti-climax implicit in final reference to food or drink, and even, fortuitously maybe, the same amusing conjunction of boys and girls!

Thus, I would suggest, some aspects of Pinter's touring-period with 'Mac' rub off on the plays: that early experience of a harassed patriarchal actor–manager, his authority somewhat weakening; the rivalries, mick-taking and in-fighting of a theatrical company on the road together; McMaster's delight in role-playing and in holding the floor with vivid circumstantial anecdotes. Pinter does not, of course, transpose a theatrical experience into a purportedly non-theatrical context because he lacks invention. Nor does he use theatrical experience, theatre life, in a directly symbolic or metaphoric way (as Pirandello does in *Six Characters in Search of An Author*). It is rather that, sensing that theatre and life have various and intimate connections, he uses parts of his early professional experience to explore his own vision of reality.

Harold Pinter left one actor–manager in 1952 and joined another, Donald Wolfit, in 1953. He thus joined the company of the actor he had idolised as a schoolboy. Donald Wolfit's Shakespearian

Company had its final triumphant season in Coronation year. It had been formed in 1937 by a man of extraordinary energy, acumen and self-confidence who possessed as an actor a primitive power of performance, relying often on the grand manner of the heroic leading man. Wolfit's powerful charisma and thrifty eye for business had enabled him to form his own company two years before the Second World War, and his zeal and missionary regard for presenting Shakespeare to the public saw to it that the company performed in the most difficult and trying years of the war. By 1953 Wolfit had received great critical acclaim for his at-times electrifying tour-de-forces playing Shakespearian and classical tragic heroes. His company, on the other hand, was generally composed of aging actor friends of limited talent, and young, inexperienced 'hopefuls' such as Pinter himself. Although they were often at the receiving end of many a barbed critical attack – even, according to Ronald Harwood, providing material for music-hall comedians – they remained for the most part intensely loyal to their employer. Harold Pinter was engaged only for the spring season in 1953, but he has remained one of Wolfit's most ardent admirers. He had much to admire. In some ways Wolfit resembled Anew McMaster: he had imposing physical stature, a varied and powerful voice, a love of the 'grand manner' of heroic acting, and a fervent, quasi-religious desire to present Shakespeare and the classical dramatists to as wide an audience as possible. Wolfit's biographer, Ronald Harwood, joined his company at the same time as Harold Pinter, at the beginning of the spring season, 1953, at the King's Theatre, Hammersmith. In his biography *Sir Donald Wolfit: His Life and Work in the Unfashionable Theatre*, Harwood attempts to sum up his feelings for his subject:

> I have never encountered anyone with Wolfit's size of person-
> ality, or anyone more unashamedly individual. I am able to
> remember well the awe in which I first held him, the terror I
> experienced in his presence both on and off the stage. . . . I
> possessed a profound respect for his energy, his determination, his
> sense of service, but above all his talent. [13]

Pinter has spoken of his own reverence for the talent of Wolfit in a television tribute to the actor entitled 'The Knight Has Been Unruly', and it is clear that he responded to him in the same way as Harwood. [14] Both Harwood and Pinter were raw young actors given only small parts by Wolfit: both had time to stand in the wings and watch the man performing at the height of his powers. Both had left RADA and found more inspiration from a menial acting-existence in the tough grind of the Shakespearian Repertory Company. Pinter had found RADA too sophisticated; Harwood similarly had found it 'sterile and lifeless . . . very like a genteel finishing school',[15] yet neither young actor was to find much real individual training for his profession under Wolfit. The actor–manager's egocentricity and arrogance, and indeed the business pressures he had to face, did not allow him much time to afford direction to the members of his company. Whatever they learned about acting had to be learned from watching their employer. Harwood is particularly perceptive and frank in this matter:

> Wolfit ignored the subtler nuances of the supporting parts. Direction was given in general terms ('you must be more evil' or 'more Noble' or 'less sympathetic') so that the particular traits of character were lost. . . . Wolfit's chief direction to his company was contained in one word he had learned in his youth: 'PACE!' 'Pace, pace, pace!' he would bellow, which was his way, as it was so many actor–managers' before him, of getting the company to speak at unnatural speed, so that he could speak more slowly. He could be brutal and bullying to those who did not obey, or who asked the fatal question 'Why?' Rehearsals revealed the darkest side of Wolfit's nature, and the worst lessons he had learned in his youth were the ones he remembered best. It was not that Wolfit's actors were bad; it was that they were never given any help to be good.[16]

Harwood more particularly remembers that Harold Pinter was often no more than a 'whipping boy' for Wolfit at the King's Theatre. After recalling that Wolfit would summon actors out of favour by surname alone, Harwood remembers an incident from the first rehearsal of *The Wandering Jew*:

> [Wolfit] glanced at the company of assembled actors and said, 'I want someone to carry the cross past the window in the first scene.' His gaze rested on one young man; with his voice at its most sonorous, Wolfit called out 'Pinter!'[17]

(In a recent interview with the author, Pinter remembered the carrying of the cross, however, as being offered as a privilege!)

In the season which lifted Wolfit to unparalleled popularity with press and general public alike – even the *Daily Express* was prompted to write of Wolfit's 'West End Glamour', and joined the *Daily Herald* and *Reynolds News* in publishing gossipy background articles about the 'Grand Old Man of the Stage' and his domestic life – Harold Pinter was a very minor figure in the company. From playing 'second leads' with Anew McMaster's company, Pinter played little more than walk-on parts. In the Shakespearian repertoire he played an Officer in *Twelfth Night*, Salanio in *The Merchant of Venice*, the Second Murderer in *Macbeth*, Nicholas in *The Taming of the Shrew* and a Knight in *King Lear*. In Sophocles's *Oedipus Rex* and *Oedipus at Colonus* (translated by E. F. Watling) he played an Elder and a Countryman, and in Temple Thurston's *The Wandering Jew* he played the Duke of Normandy and a Counsellor.

Pinter himself has written of the splendour of Wolfit's crowning performance of this season, his Oedipus, and how he, Pinter, was transfixed by a moment of sheer majesty and power that Wolfit's technique produced. Ronald Harwood writes at length of the delights of that particular virtuoso performance. The strengths of Wolfit as an actor are vividly presented as he and surely Pinter would remember:

> Wolfit's Oedipus ranked high in his achievements. As with Tamburlaine, the actor was required to undergo a gruelling test of physical endurance. The length of the roles and their sheer spiritual weight taxed Wolfit to the limits. In *Oedipus Rex* . . . Wolfit presented a stern noble tyrant; in *Oedipus at Colonus* . . . he achieved a sustained serenity of mystic beauty, his voice caressing the pain, the despair of the blinded King. Hobson, in *The Sunday Times*, detected the real technical accomplishment of the first performance, when he wrote of the actor's 'splendid grading of Oedipus's growing suspicions', for only a leading man, experienced in and tested by the classic drama, could pace himself with such expert stealth. . . . Wolfit built tension upon tension, like a cat stalking its prey. At last, when the time came to pounce, Oedipus, rocking on his heels, cried 'ANSWER!' High-pitched, staccato, brutal, he supplied a moment of vivid theatrical reality. . . .[18]

The 'moment of vivid theatrical reality' which Pinter recalled from the *Oedipus at Colonus* performances has been in no small way inspirational to him as a playwright:

one image of [Wolfit] remains with me strongly . . . he was standing high up on a rostrum with all the light on him . . . he stood with his back to the audience with a cloak round him and there came the moment when the man downstage finished his speech and we all knew, the play demanded it, the audience knew, that Wolfit or Oedipus was going to speak, was going to turn and speak. He held the moment until one's stomach was truly trembling and the cloak came round; a tremendous swish that no one else has been able to achieve I think. And the savagery and power that emerged from such a moment was extraordinary.[19]

The big theatrical moment with the aid of a prop or, in this case, a costume property was a very important part of the theatrical essence of Sir Donald Wolfit. Ronald Harwood recollects Wolfit's especial delight in obtaining props and costumes which had been passed down from one grand actor–manager to another, or, in a manner of speaking, from one Shakespearian hero to another. The whip he used as Lear or Petruchio belonged to another Lear of the grand manner, Randle Ayrton, and to Oscar Asche before him. When Sir John Martin-Harvey, a Hamlet of much renown in the 1910s and 1920s, died in 1944 Wolfit 'purchased a large quantity of costumes and effects, among them the late actor–manager's wardrobe for Oedipus which he had played in 1912. . . . By 1953, the costumes were of little use but Wolfit salvaged a gold circlet of laurel leaves that Martin-Harvey had used in the part.'[20] As will be shown later, this recognition of the importance of theatrical properties is shared, though in a different way, by Pinter the dramatist: Wolfit the actor used them and valued them as talismen or charms; Pinter conjures his own kind of powerful effect from everyday objects used in the contemporary settings of his own plays.

From Anew McMaster and Donald Wolfit then, Harold Pinter seems to have drawn a feeling for the passion, emotional intensity and sheer theatricality of drama. Both were in a sense father figures, and as such artistically influenced the impressionable young actor in their own ways. Ronald Harwood accurately defines the sort of lifestyle Pinter must have experienced under the two actor–managers:

Paternalism was at the heart of the actor–manager system. The supporting players were expected to conform to the rules of the family and the first rule was a proper deference to Father both on and off the stage. In return Father took upon himself all the burdens of a conscientious breadwinner with undisputed authority over the children. Discipline was strict but the rewards were great: security of employment, varied parts and the opportunity to watch and learn.[21]

But with Wolfit Pinter did not enjoy security of employment, since he was not retained for the autumn season. Much as he admired Wolfit as an actor, he refused to play the role of dutiful son to someone whose autocratic nature he did not find in any way paternal. In a recent interview with the present writer (19 September 1983) Pinter illustrated in some detail the friction that existed between them. He refused to be brow-beaten or bullied by his actor–manager. On one occasion, the young actor took exception to being summoned for a Sunday charity matinee performance, having been given only a few days' notice. He was the only member of Wolfit's company not to appear. Wolfit was displeased but could do little about it at the time. More tellingly, and publicly, bitter feelings were revealed in a final rehearsal for *As You Like It*, which Pinter vividly recalled to me.

Wolfit was in the stalls, directing, though also playing Touchstone; Pinter entered as Jaques de Boys in the final scene and uttered the first two lines of his part:

> Let me have audience for a word or two:
> I am the second son of old Sir Rowland

– at which point he was interrupted by his director: 'No, no, no, no! Nonsense ... This is your moment ... Give it some attack, panache. Get off and do it again!' This confrontation occurred a second time. And, at the third attempt at the speech, having been granted an audience indeed for no more than a word or two, Pinter stopped himself halfway through the second line, pre-empting a third interruption from Wolfit. Pinter deliberately exited the way he had just entered and paused amidst profound, embarrassed silence. Pinter thereupon entered a fourth time without prompting and again began the speech; he stopped after two words of his second line and made another unscripted early exit. He paused in the wings again before entering for the fifth time to deliver the speech throughout. Wolfit was unable, or unwilling, to comment. The master–servant relationship that Wolfit fostered as manager–producer had momentarily been reversed.

This personal conflict with Donald Wolfit, more serious and hostile than Pinter's struggles with Anew McMaster, may be adjudged to have had some bearing on the theme of the struggle for mastery that Pinter began to explore only two years later in the short story 'The Examination', and afterwards, as has been frequently acknowledged, in his plays.

The 'struggle' between Wolfit and Pinter was, however, short-lived, and for the next five or so years Harold Pinter was to experience the harsher struggles of a provincial repertory actor in the constant battle for work.

3 Enter David Baron

The next four years of Pinter's acting-career, from 1954 to 1958, were to be spent in provincial repertory, working, as he put it, 'all over the place'. In 1954 Pinter changed his name (professionally) to David Baron and worked intermittently in the Whitby and Huddersfield repertory companies as well as touring quite extensively with one particular play; in 1955 he played a full season at Colchester and a summer season in his favourite Ireland; in 1956 he played in Bournemouth and Torquay; in 1957 he acted in Torquay, Birmingham and Palmers Green; and in 1958 and 1959, now based in London, he played in Palmers Green and Richmond.

For the first time in his professional career Pinter was involved as an actor with the works of contemporary or near-contemporary playwrights. The early fifties in the English theatre were not the most inspiring time for the serious young actor trying to make his way in his chosen profession through the hard grind of the provincial repertories. These were to most intents and purposes a good example of Brook's Deadly Theatre, living from hand to mouth, in parasitic fashion, on the left-overs of the West End theatre. There was more than a touch of death in the air, for two main reasons: first, the competition from films, radio and, most importantly, television was proving too strong; and, secondly, the offerings provided by the West End were on the whole not fresh, intrinsically worthwhile or relevant enough to enable the repertory theatres to flourish. Although the 'play safe' policy of West End repeats was in the circumstances understandable, it did nothing to halt the decline.

The English theatre in the years immediately following the struggles and deprivations of war was content to enjoy the peace without taking too much account of the alienation, depression and loss of old values that marred the new order. Arnold Hinchliffe sums up the general theatrical scene after mentioning Kenneth Tynan's 'Notes on a Dead Language' (1955), which bemoaned the lack of any English dramatist of note since Shakespeare:

The leading dramatists of this period, like Priestley, Rattigan, Coward, Greene, Hunter and Ustinov, were writing well-constructed plays on familiar themes whose main fault, but it was a serious one, was that those themes did not correspond with the mood of frustration prevalent in the 1950s. Individuals sensed that they were caught up in some action where the causes were too large or remote to be useful either in life or the theatre.[1]

According to the dramatist R. C. Sherriff, English audiences of the post-war period went to the theatre for clever acting, an intriguing variety of scenes, fascinating actresses in eye-catching clothes.[2] It is certainly true that by the 1950s the well-made play, craftsmanlike and tidily constructed but uninventive technically and too derivative in its inspiration, formed the staple diet of theatre audiences and seemed to have lost touch with reality. Representative plays in the early 1950s were Rattigan's *The Sleeping Prince*, written for the Coronation season; N. C. Hunter's sub-Chekhovian plays, with their vaguely romantic-sounding titles, *A Day by the Sea* and *The Waters of the Moon*; Sandy Wilson's sentimental, whimsical *Salad Days* and *The Boy Friend*; some late and rather inferior Noel Coward and J. B. Priestley (*Nude with Violin* and *Mr Kettle and Mrs Moon*, for example); servicemen's comedies and farces, often paraded at the Whitehall Theatre, such as *Seagulls over Sorrento* (Hugh Hastings) and *Reluctant Heroes* (Colin Morris); and the perennial Agatha Christie thrillers, which multiplied considerably during the period in question. Most of this selection and the many plays of similar type made for reliable entertainment were competent and well crafted but safe and unadventurous, appealing to the kind of conventional and somewhat old-fashioned moral standards of Terence Rattigan's Aunt Edna figure – 'a nice respectable middle class, middle-aged maiden lady, with time on her hands, and money to help her pass it . . . a hopeless lowbrow'.[3] Although it is fair to acknowledge that Rattigan was tongue-in-cheek here, and was later dismayed to find his words used as a stick to beat him with, nevertheless the figure of Aunt Edna loomed large as an unofficial censor-figure or at least as representative of the audiences of the provincial repertory theatres, which were losing younger audiences to television and, as usual, working-class audiences to music-hall and variety shows, radio and the cinema.

However, this picture is not complete for either London or the provincial repertory theatre. In London particularly, H. M.

Tennents were associated with T. S. Eliot's verse dramas, while the stylistically original plays of Christopher Fry and John Whiting were occasionally presented in the West End. A commercial impresario, Donald Albery, afforded Beckett's revolutionary *Waiting for Godot*, from Paris, its first London production at the Criterion in 1955. The theatres of the capital also successfully accommodated a number of vital and exciting plays from America and Europe. Arthur Miller's *A View from the Bridge*, *All My Sons* and *The Crucible*, Tennessee Williams's *Cat on a Hot Tin Roof*, and plays by Giraudoux and Anouilh became known to London audiences in the early 1950s – all of them perhaps dealing more searchingly and truthfully with human relationships than the majority of contemporary English plays. The occasional example of this more enterprising fare is to be found in some provincial repertory programmes. Pinter played in Eliot's *The Confidential Clerk* and Anouilh's *Point of Departure* at Colchester in 1955, and *All My Sons* was on the Birmingham Repertory's list of plays for 1957. But on the whole the theatre of safe 'well-made' dramas was even more deeply entrenched in the provinces than in London. And Pinter's only contact with Beckett's work in the 1950s came through his reading of the Irishman's earlier novels when touring with Anew McMaster in Ireland. The companies Pinter worked for believed for the most part in the value of reproducing as faithfully and as swiftly as possible recent West End successes, and doggedly attempted to woo middle-class provincial audiences away from the cinema and the television.

Norman Marshall expressed his horror at the working-conditions experienced by repertory actors in the post-war period. He complains bitterly in an article on repertory theatres written in 1947, when the reps were comparatively flourishing, that

> the 'weekly rep' is having a deplorable effect on the standard of English acting and production. It is literally impossible to rehearse a play properly in a week, especially when only a small part of the day can be devoted to rehearsals. An actor playing long seasons in repertory cannot go on for month after month rehearsing morning and afternoon, playing in the evenings, learning his lines when he can snatch a few minutes to himself. So the usual routine in a repertory theatre is to rehearse in the morning only, with the company given one day off to learn their lines. The average time spent on the rehearsal of a play by a

weekly repertory company, excluding the dress rehearsal, is fifteen hours.[4]

It was this sort of pressurised lifestyle that bred the typical 'rep actor', who 'acquired tricks which will enable him to get through a part even when he scarcely knows it'.[5]

In 1953 the Theatre Book Club published Richard Findlater's *The Unholy Trade*. In his chapter 'Masks and Faces' Findlater points to the limiting factors in an English actor's experience: the prevalent 'Oxford' or BBC voice, and 'the pigeonholing of other ways of speech as "character parts" and "dialects"'. Findlater points to the source of much of this pigeonholing as being the repertory experience of most English actors:

> The parts . . . are usually stock roles, for most companies present a selection of West End long runners and popular stand-bys – Ian Hay, Terence Rattigan, A. A. Milne, Esther McCracken – interspersed with an occasional sally into Ibsen, Shaw or Shakespeare, too brief and hasty to do much more than whet the good player's appetite for more.[6]

The very nature of the stereotyped plays presented by repertory companies encouraged typecasting in every rank of English theatre both before and after the war.

Findlater is especially perceptive on this point, condemning typecasting as 'one of the most pernicious practices of the modern theatre . . . fostered both by the players and the managers', and he instances such popular 'types' as 'Scottish character', 'Cockney char' and even 'Happy Hubby'. To a certain extent the older-established notions of 'walking gentlemen', 'light juvenile', 'heavy' and 'other stand-bys' were in decline, but 'all parts were played in the same way'.[7]

In the same article Findlater exposes the meagre life of the contemporary English actor:

> Most of Britain's eleven thousand mummers enjoy a seventy-hour working week in the provinces, at rates of pay well below the general professional levels. The minimum wage is still only £4 compared with the national average of £6 5s. and working conditions backstage in most provincial playhouses would not be

tolerated by good trade unionists in self-respecting factories and offices. . . . Acting is one of the few occupations in a planned economy where unemployment is not only common but encouraged. Most actors are drudges on the treadmill of weekly repertory, spending every evening on the boards and every day in rehearsals. [8]

Ronald Hayman's later study of the theatrical scene, *The Set Up*, adds further detail to the depressing picture of provincial repertory conditions. The actor's salary had gone up slightly but so no doubt had prices and the general standard of living, and, as Hayman says, in the late 1950s 'actors were mostly paid salaries quite close to the minimum, which was £6 10s. 0d. a week'. [9] In 1958–9, he says, only twenty-two out of the seventy-four companies were receiving portions of a £44,500 grant. It is unlikely that any of the repertory companies Pinter acted in received such grants. And, in any case, Arts Council grants and financial help from local authorities came too late to save many of these struggling repertory companies in the 1950s. By 1957 many were closing and others followed in the years immediately afterwards, so that by 1973, the year of publication of Hayman's report, only forty-five repertories remained and, despite being subsidised, were still not commercially viable. Hayman sums up the policy of the typical weekly repertory company at the time of Pinter's involvement with them:

There were six fortnightly repertories – the Bristol Little, the Birmingham Alexandra, Hornchurch, Ipswich, Nottingham and Sheffield. And apart from summer seasons, there were seventy-four weekly repertory companies in England, eight of which were performing twice nightly. . . . For giving twelve performances each week (as well as rehearsing next week's play and learning lines) actors were paid the twice-nightly minimum of £7 10s. 0d. Some good productions were done in the better repertories and even, occasionally, in the weekly ones, but there was too little time and too little money for high standards to be maintained. The plays were mostly well-tried London successes, and some directors depended heavily on French's Acting Editions, which often contained detailed stage directions copied from the West End prompt book. What the provincial audiences were seeing were reproductions of stage business that had been effective in London. [10]

The repertory companies also had to compete – especially in the seaside towns – with music-hall and variety-show entertainment provided by such comics as Arthur Askey and Frankie Howerd. Leslie Smith, in research into Pinter's acting-career, has pointed out the proximity of the legitimate and illegitimate theatres in seaside resorts in the 1950s:

> In the Spring and Summer of 1956, for instance, while David Baron was playing at the Palace Court, Arthur Askey, Tommy Trinder, Dave King, Jimmy Edwards, Charlie Chester, Max Bygraves, Sam Costa and Frankie Howerd were some of the variety stars to be found at the Winter Garden or New Royal Theatre in Bournemouth.[11]

At the same time, the medium of radio, with which Pinter had already been professionally associated, afforded much in the way of comic talent, involving most of these leading comedians mentioned, together with Tony Hancock; Al Read; the master of the quickfire comic monologue, Arthur English; and double acts such as Jimmy James and his various stooges ('Our Eli', for example) and Jimmy Jewel and Ben Warriss. Hancock and Read had successful radio shows of their own, whilst the others mainly appeared on radio variety programmes such as *Mid-day Music Hall* and *Worker's Playtime*. Television too was an ever-growing serious competitor in the fight to win audiences. Like radio it provided a medium for much comic talent. Harry H. Corbett, who fulfilled his acting-ambitions playing Harold Steptoe in the 1960s, was a repertory actor during the 1950s and points to one possible reason why the repertory companies were failing to compete successfully with television:

> I looked at TV and all I saw that was making any kind of good . . . social comment was the Hancocks, the Eric Sykes', this kind of half-hour comedy programme. Oh, I did envy them . . . the work done by people like Hancock, Sykes, Bentine and a few more is a great period and in so many years' time it will be revived as a classic period of really fantastic social comment.[12]

In many ways the best of such entertainment, as Corbett suggests, offered a more vital kind of theatre than the diet of West End repeats offered by provincial repertory companies. Michael Billington refs to the dominance, in some of Pinter's works, of techniques used by music-hall comedians and even vaudeville artistes,[13] and, as will be suggested later, Pinter, whose writing in this period involved at least one revue sketch, does owe something to this popular tradition. Indeed, in an interview he told me that he frequently went to the music hall as a child, and that among his favourite comedians were Al Read, Max Miller, and the Marx Brothers.

Pinter's references to his repertory-theatre experiences are few in number, and not particularly specific or detailed, as has already been noted:

> I saw very few plays, in fact, before I was twenty. Then I acted in too many ... I've worked all over the place in reps – Huddersfield, Torquay, Bournemouth, Whitby, Colchester, Birmingham, Chesterfield, Worthing, Palmers Green and Richmond. I was an actor for about nine years (under the name of David Baron) and I would like to do more.[14]

In an interview with Laurence M. Bensky – first published in the *Paris Review* in 1966 – Pinter offers a graphic account of the occasional squalor of theatrical digs. He is speaking of the sources for *The Room* and *The Birthday Party*:

> *The Birthday Party* had also been in my mind for a long time. It was sparked off from a very distinct situation in digs when I was on tour. In fact the other day a friend of mine gave me a letter I wrote to him in nineteen fifty something, Christ knows when it was. This is what it says, 'I have filthy insane digs, a great bulging scrag of a woman, with breasts rolling at her belly, an obscene household, cats, dogs, filth, tea-strainers, mess, oh bollocks, talk, chat rubbish shit scratch dung poison, infantility, deficient order in the upper fretwork, fucking roll on . . . .' Now the thing about this is *that* was *The Birthday Party* – I was in those digs, and this woman was Meg in the play, and there was a fellow staying there in Eastbourne, on the coast. The whole thing remained with me, and three years later I wrote the play.[15]

Later in the same interview Pinter replies to a question about whether he had considered acting in *The Room*:

> No, no – the acting was a separate activity altogether. Though I

wrote *The Room*, *The Birthday Party*, and *The Dumb Waiter* in 1957, I was acting all the time in a repertory company, doing all kinds of jobs, travelling to Bournemouth and Torquay and Birmingham. I finished *The Birthday Party* while I was touring in some kind of farce, I don't remember the name.[16]

In a much later interview, with Melvyn Bragg in 1978,[17] he added the information that he was in fact touring in *Doctor in the House*, to Leicester and other places, at the time in question. He also referred to appearing in *Ten Little Niggers* and *Separate Tables*, and earlier in his acting-career in the lesser-known play *A Horse! A Horse!* in Eastbourne. In one of the very few references to parts played he recalled circumstances in which he remet his wife to be:

> After two years in Ireland, I got a job with Donald Wolfit's Shakespearean company where I met my wife. We didn't get to know each other very well then, but we met again, in 1956, in the Bournemouth Repertory Company. . . . I was the leading man, and we played opposite each other. She played Jane Eyre and I played Rochester and that year we got married.[18]

In this interview given in 1967 he gave a most detailed account of his early life but again was most sparing in references to his experiences as a repertory actor, and again failed to offer any real comment on the plays he acted in or the repertory experience as a whole.

Harold Pinter was often, especially early on in his career, out of work as an actor and spent some time in casual temporary work as a caretaker, a waiter, a street hawker, a doorman at a dance hall, a door-to-door book salesman, a dishwasher and a snow-shoveller.[19] Some aspects of this experience have been used in plays such as *The Caretaker*, in which the titular role is painstakingly defined by the leading characters, and *The Homecoming*, which contains Lennie's snow-shovelling story. In some of his early poetry Pinter hints at the low quality of life he experienced as a repertory actor:

> Now here again she blows, landlady of lumping
> Fellows between the boards,
> Singing 'O Celestial Light' while
> Like a T-square on the
> Flood swings her wooden leg.
> This is the shine, the powder and blood, and here am I,

Straddled, exile always in one Whitbread Ale town, or
such.[20]

Of his experience of the various kinds of repertory he writes, in a
sombre vein,

> So March has become a museum,
> And the April curtains move.
> I travel the vacant gallery
> To the last seat. . . .
> The actors pitch tents. . . .
> Their cries in the powdered dark
> Assemble in mourning over
> Ambassadors from the wings . . . .
> I move to the interval,
> Done with this repertory.[21]

In another poem, 'The Second Visit', Pinter compares a childhood
recollection of a seaside place with the more painful adult
experience of it:

> My childhood vampire wallows in those days,
> Where panting sea threatened and surf was flint,
> And consummate doves flanked the eyes.
>
> Now an actor in this nocturnal sink,
> The strip of lip is toothed away,
> And flats and curtains canter down.[22]

The latent violence that is somehow implicit in the life of the
struggling actor was to manifest itself in an outburst of violence
when Pinter was in London working as a repertory actor. Pinter has
described a fight he had in a Chelsea pub after being racially
insulted:

> I laid into him, forgetting who he was and what the whole thing
> was about entirely. I just kept on and on. Afterwards I thought
> one has a lot of physical energy. . . . I wasn't insulted personally
> but I was insulted on behalf of someone or something . . . .[23]

Pinter's excessive display of violence was recalled later by a witness,

the playwright Alun Owen, who at the time of the incident –
1957–8 – was in a similar situation: 'We were both acting and writing
when we first met.' Owen retells the incident as Pinter remembered
it and adds, 'When things calmed down, this bloke said to Harold:
"Are you a Jew?" He said yes and the other fellow said curiously, 'In
that case I can understand why you hit me. But why did you go *on*
hitting me?'[24] Pinter, however, has recently affirmed that the man
actually said, 'But why did you hit me so hard?', and has suggested
that the incident has little to do with himself as an actor but more
with himself as a man.[25] Nevertheless, from these reminiscences and
recollections, poetic and otherwise, one receives a picture of the
tensions and frustrations Pinter felt, and the tough, rather squalid
conditions he often endured as a repertory actor. It might be fairly
assumed that generally Pinter was not at his happiest in this period
of his life, although he is not prepared to state anything unequivo-
cally on the matter: 'When I was a failure I wasn't a failure to me.
When I'm a success, I'm not a success to me. I'm not gloomy about
it. I'm not a gloomy person . . . but in some ways I am.'[26]

Pinter began playing in repertory in June 1954 in Whitby's Spa
Theatre. He had rejoined Anew McMaster for several months
shortly after leaving Wolfit's company in the summer of 1953. He
then returned to England in search of theatrical work, and after
several unsuccessful attempts to secure a position with a repertory
company he decided to adopt a stage name. This decision followed
the advice of a theatrical agent, who assured Pinter that his name
was preventing him from getting a job: 'You'll never get anywhere
as Harold Pinter.' Consequently, the young actor took upon himself
the stage name 'David Baron'. 'Baron' sounded more imposing and
served its purpose. It was the name of a character in an early
novel that Pinter has not had published.

The engagement at Whitby, however, was short-lived, despite its
promise: he was straightaway given two leading roles, one in *Murder
in the Vicarage* by Agatha Christie, and the other in the farce *Here We
Come Gathering*, by Philip King and A. Armstrong. He resigned
following a row with the manager, a local butcher. He had sacked a
young assistant stage-manager on the recommendation of her
landlady, who had reported her for staying out beyond a respectable hour. It was generally known that she was romantically
involved with the new leading man, who insisted on being treated in
exactly the same manner as the lady in question. The butcher–
manager refused to reinstate her; Pinter promptly resigned and

returned to London on the next train, without being able to buy a
ticket. As he was met by police at King's Cross, the words of his
previous employer were still ringing in his ears: 'You'll never work
in the theatre again.'

One month later, however, David Baron was himself working as
an assistant stage-manager, manipulating the head of a talking
horse and uttering one line himself in a Hugh Wakefield-led farce, *A
Horse! A Horse!*, which began a tour in Eastbourne. Despite getting a
name check in *The Stage*,[27] Pinter only closely avoided dismissal
after failing in one performance to make the horse 'speak'; later,
after a short period of unemployment, he returned northwards, to
Huddersfield, to play in two comedies, *Affairs of State* by Louis
Verneuil and *Late Love* by Rosemary Casey, and the Agatha Christie
thriller *Ten Little Niggers*.

The following year, 1955, saw Pinter established as a repertory
actor playing a fair number of leading parts, specialising in 'heavy'
villains and 'straight' conventional leading-man roles. He played in
Colchester from the end of February to the beginning of December
of that year, with a break in midsummer when he returned to
Ireland, with members of the company, for a short season at Port
Stewart. The Colchester company, like most of their repertory
counterparts, mainly featured West End light comedies and
thrillers in their programme, but varied this diet with the occasional
American play, such as John Steinbeck's *Of Mice and Men* (adapted
from the novel) and George Axelrod's *Seven Year Itch*, and even the
odd less obviously commercial piece such as Anouilh's *Point of
Departure* (based on the Orpheus myth) and Graham Greene's *The
Living Room*.

In 1956 Harold Pinter had a most successful season playing many
leading roles with the Barry O'Brien Company at the Palace Court,
Bournemouth. It was in this year that he married Vivien Merchant.
In the first four plays of the spring season Pinter took the leading
romantic role in two dramas taken from the works of female
novelists, *Jane Eyre* and *Rebecca*, and in two lighter romantic
comedies that had been recently staged in London, Alan Melville's
Simon and Laura and Peter Blackmore's *Mad about Men*. Later in the
season Pinter played in the usual repertory mixture of comedies and
thrillers, including the then-famous role of the maniacal killer in
Frank Vosper's adaptation of Agatha Christie's *Love from a Stranger*,
and the role of a bank-manager-turned-rebel in J. B. Priestley's *Mr
Kettle and Mrs Moon*. It is perhaps worth noting that the

Bournemouth Repertory Company was a thriving concern in the year of Pinter's first marriage, when also he gained a promising reputation as an actor. *The Stage* featured a most favourable review of the season at Bournemouth:

> Barry O'Brien and his co-director Michael Hamilton have reason to congratulate themselves. In addition to their highly successful season at Shanklin and Ryde the Bournemouth company have been breaking all previous records at the Palace Court and house full boards have been out regularly. Guy Vassen is resident producer and the company includes Vivien Merchant, David Baron . . . . Some of the most successful productions have been *The Shadow of Doubt*, *The Tender Trap*, *Mr Kettle and Mrs Moon*, and *Ring for Catty*. David Baron and Vivien Merchant . . . are to be married on September 14th.[28]

One would, however, be well advised at this point to take note of a comment made by the then box-office manager at the Palace Court. She strongly asserted that the real 'star' of the season was Vivien Merchant, and that David Baron, although of striking appearance and at times emotionally powerful, was inclined to be rather too detached – 'as if he were looking on at the whole thing'.[29]

In the autumn and winter of 1956 and 1957 Pinter worked for Philip Barrett's New Malvern Company in Torquay. The plays in the repertory were much like those in Bournemouth, but also included Rattigan's *Separate Tables* and Coward's *South Sea Bubble*. After this Pinter toured the country with a production of *Doctor in the House*, a popular farce based on the Richard Gordon books. During these early and middle months of 1957 *The Room* was written in haste, on the promise that it would be staged at Bristol University by a friend, Henry Woolf, and was shortly followed by *The Dumb Waiter* and *The Birthday Party*. In the summer and autumn of 1957 Pinter played in a handful of plays at the Alexandra Theatre, Birmingham, for the well-established repertory company there. Vivien Merchant was in Coward's *Hay Fever*, whilst her husband appeared in Agatha Christie's *Spider's Web* (for the second time), R. C. Sherriff's *The Telescope* and Arthur Miller's *All My Sons*. Subsequently Pinter and his wife became more or less permanently based in London. He appeared in Fred Tripp's company, based at the Intimate Theatre, Palmers Green, playing a couple of police detectives in thrillers, and most notably, perhaps, Cliff Lewis in a production of John

Osborne's *Look Back in Anger*. In April 1958 Pinter was understudy-
ing at the Royal Court for two N. F. Simpson plays, *A Resounding
Tinkle* and *The Hole*. It was during this month that *The Birthday Party*
was first produced, at the Arts Theatre, Cambridge, prior to its brief
run at the Lyric Theatre, Hammersmith. David Baron continued
his career at the Richmond Theatre, playing in a pair of
conventional dramas, one an American comedy, and the other *Any
Other Business*, which concerned itself with the power struggles
inherent in the world of provincial commerce. The latter play he
played in again, a month later, in Worthing under rather taxing
circumstances. *The Birthday Party* had not been a commercial
success; Pinter had sacrificed a comparatively lucrative contract
with the Birmingham Rep (which also wanted the services of his
wife, Vivien Merchant) to stay in London to keep an eye on his own
play; there was the additional complication of a recently arrived
baby son, and thus, needing a regular weekly wage, Pinter was
grateful for the offer of a couple of small parts with the Worthing
company, whose producer, Guy Vaesen, he had worked with at
Bournemouth in 1956. After the first night of *Any Other Business* the
leading actor, Gerald Flood, fell ill and David Baron stepped into
the breach at twenty-four hours' notice to play the part he had
recently performed at Richmond. For thus saving the show Pinter
was rewarded by the management – he vividly remembers – with a
£1 note pressed gratefully into his hands. After performing in a
Thornton Wilder comedy he returned to London.

   During the following year, 1959, he played in the occasional
repertory play at Richmond, most notably as Marco in Arthur
Miller's *A View From the Bridge*, and as Corporal Johnstone in Willis
Hall's *The Long and the Short and the Tall*. Harold Pinter the
playwright finally caught up with David Baron the actor at
Cheltenham's Theatre Royal in September 1960. Pinter decided to
kill off his stage name when he realised the incongruity of the
billboard announcement: 'David Baron and Patrick Magee in *The
Birthday Party* by Harold Pinter.' Thus David Baron the repertory
actor ended his career as Harold Pinter the playwright, and Harold
Pinter the occasional television, film and stage actor came into
international prominence.

What kind of an actor, then, was David Baron? During these
repertory years he acquired a reputation as someone who could

sustain a leading role, and win the attention of audiences and local critics alike. The varied styles of repertory play ensured that Pinter would be called upon to play many different types of role. Yet, as had been noted by Richard Findlater[30] and others, certain stock roles kept on recurring in a repertoire which included so many light comedies, farces and romances apparently written to a formula. Harold Pinter, in fact, might be said to have successfully performed in roles which at the time could have been classified as 'heavy', 'romantic lead' and 'sophisticated character'. From an extensive study of the reviews of relevant local newspapers it can be gathered, interestingly enough, that Pinter was at his best either in deeply emotional roles or in sinister 'heavy' parts. It is perhaps worth adding that the only role Pinter has recalled from his repertory experience combined the elements of emotional depth and the sinister – namely, that of Rochester in *Jane Eyre*, which he played at the beginning of his most successful year of acting, in Bournemouth. His performance was indeed considered as something above par for the repertory course:

> There emerges a characterisation of Samson strength. We have never this season seen David Baron in so forthright a performance. His Rochester is a solid achievement in a Repertory world so often content with milk and water performances.[31]

Now, Dorothy Brandon's stage adaptation of Charlotte Bronte's nineteenth-century novel may seem a far cry from the world of Harold Pinter's plays, but there does exist a link in the air of mystery and menace which surrounds the character of Rochester, much as it surrounds many a Pinter character. Hirst in *No Man's Land* is indeed an enigmatic figure, and may, for all Spooner or the audience knows, be another Rochester! 'Is she here now, your wife? Cowering in a locked room, perhaps?' (p. 31).*

Immediately after the role of Rochester in the spring of 1956 came that of Mr de Winter in Daphne du Maurier's adaptation of her novel *Rebecca*. Again the accent was on romance and enigma, and once more David Baron, appropriately playing opposite his future wife, received a favourable notice as 'a strong lead'. In all, Pinter played about eight young lovers and as many 'straight' husbands in various plays. In Jean Anouilh's *Point of Departure* he

* Page references are to editions listed on p. 138.

played a modern-day Orpheus with successful 'intensity'. He was a young airman–adventurer in *A Woman's Place* by W. Grimwood, for which he won a rather back-handed compliment: 'David Baron shapes a Marlon Brando frame into the role of adventure-struck Anthony Pett.'[32]

Pinter could also win some critical attention from his playing of light-hearted and light-headed husbands in farces such as *All for Mary* by Harold Brooke and Kay Bannerman, and Walter Ellis's *Almost a Honeymoon*. In the former Pinter played an Englishman abroad, worried by being bed-ridden whilst possible Continental rivals made romantic advances to his wife: 'Humphrey Miller, the naive husband, was admirably played by David Baron, who extracted every possible laugh line his lines offered.' In the latter play 'David Baron [did] a creditable variety turn by entangling himself in various items of bedroom furniture'.[33]

Pinter also managed to achieve some success in the playing of sundry sophisticated characters – from artists and authors to Egyptologists and medical researchers. His first recorded notice as a repertory actor was included in the review section of the *Whitby Gazette* early in 1954; Pinter had appeared as the murderer in Agatha Christie's *Murder at the Vicarage*: 'David Baron was assured as the sophisticated artist, mixing charm and ruthlessness to bring the character always in focus.'[34] At Colchester the following year he played an impressive lead in the romantic comedy *Down Came a Blackbird*: 'Mr Baron's bearded Sir Clive (an Egyptologist romantically fought over by two rivals) is just the sort to send shivers of excitement down the spines of TV panel game viewers.' Obviously, Pinter had brought a certain sensational popular appeal to what is a rather straightforward, fairly suave but mainly cultivated character. Later that year Pinter was to play a middle-aged would-be seducer in F. Hugh Herbert's *The Moon is Blue*. Pinter's performance brought out, according to the local reviewer, the 'devilish charm' of the character of the 'naughty rich gent'. He also proved himself adept in the role of sophisticated and charming American political agent Byron Winkler in a romantic comedy equivocally called *Affairs of State*. Later, he played another sophisticated stock role, an author enthused by witchcraft and the black arts, in John Van Druten's *Bell, Book and Candle*:

David Baron, as a more than usually prosperous caricature of a writer fascinated by the black art, is less well served by the playwright. The part is comparatively small and offers little scope for the actor's art – but again first impressions are intriguing.

In the many whodunnit and mystery plays that Pinter played in it was often in the role of the policeman or inspector that he made his mark. During his repertory career Pinter played the whole range: Inspector, Police Constable, Detective Sergeant, Police Inspector, Plain Clothes Detective, Detective Constable, CID Inspector and MI5 Man. It was a successful kind of typecasting: 'MI5 is at the door in the person of David Baron, black from homburg to toe-cap, a forbidding figure warning the doctors of science of the wrath to come.' Thus is Pinter described, perhaps in rather tongue-in-cheek fashion, by the reviewer of Bournemouth Repertory's version of Norman King's political thriller *The Shadow of Doubt*. In *The Golden Earring*, described as 'a new murder mystery by Naomi Waters', 'David Baron gives the best all round performance of the evening . . . as a suave member of the CID.' He played two roles in different productions of *The Whole Truth*: one a detective, and one a murderer pretending to be a detective! At both he was successful; first at Bournemouth ('I confess I was a little disturbed by David Baron's playing. I have never seen him inject so much of the insidious into a role') and secondly in Torquay ('David Baron in a key role makes an impressive entrance as the almost too charming detective sergeant who arrives to break the news'). By 1958 Harold Pinter had become very impressive in the role of detective. He received a most interesting and revealing notice for his performance in Ian Main's *Subway in the Sky*:

> but the outstanding acting success in the play is David Baron's plain-clothes 'dick'. With his half-ingratiating, half-cynical smile, his lazy, or suddenly swift, cat-like movement, he is beautifully in character every moment and suggests all the possibilities of a coiled spring.

Pinter seemingly had a fine talent most especially for manic and psychotic roles and received two outstanding notices for performances of this variety. He twice played the maniacal killer in the classic Agatha Christie thriller *Love from a Stranger*. On the second occasion he received the following praise:

> David Baron [was] suitably sinister . . . the play culminates in a

climax of almost explosive intensity with David Baron attacking his macabre part with a ferocity which would have done justice to the Grand Guignol.

Obviously Pinter was capable of giving a melodramatic role the full theatrical treatment! The other role concerned with mental derangement might arguably, as will be seen later, have created a deep impression on Pinter the playwright. In the Colchester *Essex County Standard* appears the following review of a play now sadly out of print, Mary Hayley Bell's *The Uninvited Guest*:

> Candy is the elder son of Lady Lannion. He was certified at the age of fourteen and twenty years afterwards by his own efforts is released from the institution. . . . David Baron . . . is this uninvited guest. He . . . keeps our interest very effectively and fully exploits the mystery and strangeness of the part; . . . he conveys well the movements and attitude of a man who has been set free after being imprisoned in this way.

The list of menacing intruders and interrogators which David Baron played is indeed quite extensive, and the number of such roles must have had its effect in the creation of the intruder figures in Pinter's plays. Harold Pinter has, in a letter to the present writer, concluded a brief résumé of his acting-career with the information that he specialised in 'sinister parts'.[35]

Despite such an obvious talent for macabre roles, Pinter, whether by accident or design, did not become typecast as many a repertory actor did, and towards the end of his repertory career won favourable notices for his playing of 'straight' parts. These included a 'human and convincing'[36] Chris, the idealistic son of the pragmatic Joe Keller in Arthur Miller's *All My Sons*; a parson 'played finely and believably' from a Rattigan-style play of conscience and morality by R. C. Sherriff, *The Telescope*; a young schoolmaster in the farcical comedy *A Worm's Eye View* by R. F. Delderfield, played with 'underlying seriousness of purpose'; 'an authoritative and strong-willed administrator' in G. Ross and C. Singer's play about North Country businessmen, *Any Other Business*; 'a distressed but methodically minded husband' in a lesser-known American comedy called *The Rocky Road*; and, finally, the aforementioned role of Cliff in John Osborne's *Look Back in Anger*:

David Baron gives a real gem of a performance as Cliff. Unlettered, uncouth, understanding by instinct, friendly by nature, his Cliff Lewis is created so naturally as to add enormously to our acceptance of the thing as a whole.

4 Rep Plays and Pinter Plays

Although Pinter has had little to say in particular terms about how his years in rep have affected his play-writing, he has made a number of general comments on the subject in the interview with Richard Findlater cited at the beginning of Chapter 1. Pinter points to what he considers fundamental influences upon him as a playwright:

> Yes, my experience as an actor has influenced my plays – it must have – though it's impossible for me to put my finger on it exactly. I think I certainly developed some feeling for construction which, believe it or not, is important to me, and for speakable dialogue. I had a pretty good notion in my earlier plays of what would shut an audience up; not so much what would make them laugh; that I had no ideas about. Whenever I write for the stage I merely see the stage I've been used to. I have worked for theatre in the round and enjoyed it, but it doesn't move me to write plays with that method in mind. I always think of the normal picture-frame stage which I used as an actor. [1]

In an interview with *New Theatre Magazine* the same year, Pinter was asked if his ten years' acting-experience had conditioned his writing:

> Yes. I write pretty meticulously, and when I reach the last draft, I carefully work out the movements as I visualise them, and the pauses too. The thing must be capable of realisation, and it must work visually for me . . . . I always write in direct relation to the visual image of people walking about and standing on the stage. [2]

Five years later, in his interview with Laurence Bensky, Pinter still insists at some length on his following certain conventions as a dramatist:

I am a very traditional playwright – for instance I insist on having a curtain in all my plays. I write curtain lines for that reason. And even when directors like Peter Hall or Claude Rézy in Paris want to do away with them, I insist they stay. For me everything has to do with shape, structure and overall unity. All this jamboree in 'Happenings' and eight hour movies is great fun for the people concerned I'm sure . . . .[3]

In the same interview he displays a traditional concern for observing the hierarchical line of control from author and director through to actor: 'I don't at all believe in the anarchic theatre of so-called "creative" actors – the actors can do that in someone else's plays.'[4]

Later still, the practical man of the workaday rep emerges in statements on the subject of getting a play ready for performance:

If I am to talk at all I prefer to talk practically about practical matters. . . . I distrust theory. In whatever capacity I have worked in the theatre, and apart from writing, I have done quite a bit of acting and a certain amount of directing for the stage, I have found that theory, as such, has never been helpful. . . . A rehearsal period which consists of philosophical discourse or political treatise does not get the curtain up at 8 o'clock.[5]

It is clear from these statements, first, that Pinter is hostile to what he would regard as the anarchic improvisation of 'happenings' and 'all that jamboree'. This may reflect his experience of the rigorous cut-and-dried conditions of repertory work (no possibility there for improvisation, for lengthy rehearsal, for exploratory soul-searchings) and perhaps also the influence of those patriarchal actor–manager figures, Wolfit and McMaster. Secondly, and more positively, Pinter acknowledges that his experience of rep helped him to develop 'some feeling for construction, for speakable dialogue'; and he writes of the importance for him of 'everything that has to do with shape, structure, overall unity'. In that respect he claims to be 'very traditional', and he instances the curtain line as an example of his traditionalism.

This concern for construction, for 'everything that has to do with shape, structure and overall unity', does indeed suggest that Pinter felt he had learnt something from repertory plays, though the

parenthetical 'believe it or not' in the first quotation suggests that
what is unlike may be more important than what is like. Learning
from other plays does not necessarily mean direct imitation, since
experience of other dramatists' sometimes rather contrived structures may have led him to evolve structures of his own.
Resemblances of theme and situation between Pinter's plays and
the typical rep offering may certainly be noticed. The grilling of
witnesses and cross-examination of suspects characteristic of such
detective plays as Agatha Christie's *Spider's Web* and Jack
Popplewell's *Dead on Nine* feature, in different style, in the interrogation scenes of *The Birthday Party*, *The Hothouse* and *The Caretaker*; the
introduction of a fiancé or spouse into the family home, as in Paul
Osborn's *Mornings at Seven* and Max Rietman's *Love on the Never-Never*,
is used by Pinter in *The Homecoming*; the polite banalities,
sophisticated small talk and verbal gamesmanship, often accompanied by the dispensing of drinks, found in such sophisticated
comedies as Rosemary Casey's *Late Love*, F. Hugh Herbert's *The
Moon is Blue* and Noel Coward's *Present Laughter* appear again in *No
Man's Land*, *A Slight Ache* and *Old Times*; the eternal-triangle
theme prominent in so many romantic comedies and dramas, such
as Ronald Miller's *Waiting for Gillian*, Joan Morgan's *Doctor Jo* and
Wendy Grimwood's *A Woman's Place*, is present in new guises in *The
Lover*, *The Collection* and *Old Times*. An examination of one such play
may serve to highlight the likeness and significant unlikeness
between the Pinter play and its repertory counterpart. The
distinctive nature of Pinter's handling of structure may also be seen
if we look at his handling of what in the vocabulary of the well-made
play would be termed the exposition.

Old Times provides a good example. It has a very satisfying
'shape, structure and overall unity', but of a very different kind from
the conventional well-made play. This may be seen if it is compared
to a repertory play to which it bears a superficial resemblance in
content, a play in which Pinter appeared as the male lead in 1956 –
Doctor Jo by Joan Morgan. In the Pinter play Kate and Deeley, a
married couple, are visited by Anna, an old friend of Kate's who, it
appears, has also known Deeley twenty years earlier. *Old Times* is
basically a series of conversations between the three of them, mostly
on the subject of the past, and attempts are made to define the
nature of the relationship that existed and gradually came to exist
between them. The conversations lead to an awareness of the
distances that separate them. *Doctor Jo* is concerned with a visit to a

country general practitioner and his narrow-minded wife by her more adventurous sister Jo, who has earned some fame internationally as a doctor, having failed to marry the GP. By means of a series of dialogues involving the three main characters, the play investigates the possibility of a relationship between the GP and Jo, but the final act ends with the withdrawal of Jo and a deepening awareness, felt by the GP in particular, of the gulfs separating the three of them. In both *Doctor Jo* and *Old Times*, then, a woman visits a married couple after a lapse of years; the visitor has had a close relationship with the wife and there has been and might still be a close relationship between the visitor and the husband. In both plays the man is left with a sense of separation from both women. At the same time there is a significant unlikeness. *Doctor Jo* begins conventionally with the telephone ringing in the middle-class drawing-room, and gradually the truth about the main characters' past lives is revealed via conversations they have with each other and with minor characters. There is an exploration of the conflicting themes of romantic enterprise and staid provincialism and an additional theme of the possibility of the past repeating itself in the future through the next generation's actions. The concentration on themes may be said to produce stereotyped characters as mere representatives of ideas. Pinter's play begins much more imaginatively and unusually with the past already gathered into the present through the shadowy figure of Anna silhouetted against the window. When at a particular moment she walks from the dimly lit backstage area into the middle of a conversation between husband and wife, her sudden appearance is not just 'effective theatre' but also expresses a feeling or idea which is important to the play – namely, that of the past and the present coexisting, affecting each other, subject alike to reinterpretation and renegotiation. Pinter's play attempts no ordered, chronological narrative sequence. It is focused on the three characters as, in exploring their past, they seek to define their present. Stylistically, therefore, *Old Times* may be seen as a much more experimental play than *Doctor Jo*, although both in their own way treat their similar themes in a tightly unified dramatic structure.

None the less, it must be observed that earlier plays of Pinter's have a less experimental construction. For example, *The Birthday Party*, in its three-act framework of exposition, development–climax and resolution, could be said to approximate to many of the well-made plays in which Pinter acted; but the total effect of the play is, of course, very unlike that of a typical example of the post-war English realistic theatre.

The difference is particularly noticeable in the case of the exposition. The gradual unfolding of the situation, the revelation of facts vital to the development are traditionally recognised features of the well-made play. One straightforward example which may be cited here is Jack Popplewell's thriller *The Vanity Case*. The police detective in this play is present at the scene of the murder from curtain-up and spends the first scene interviewing each member of the cast, thus giving the audience an apparently clear-cut presentation of the dramatist's subject-matter. Information is then carefully weighed and logically or intuitively the murderer is revealed. Such presentation, however, proceeds on the assumption that the characters have a verifiable past history, while for Pinter 'the desire for verification is understandable but cannot always be satisfied'.[6] Pinter's expositions, therefore, are of a rather different kind: the boarding-house of *The Birthday Party* does have a landlady and a guest who is leading a miserable and unfulfilled existence, but questions as to exactly who Stanley is or what he represents are as unanswerable by the audience as by Mrs Boles: 'Tell me, Mrs Boles, when you address yourself to me, do you ever ask yourself who exactly you are talking to? Eh?' (p. 31).

It must be acknowledged that Pinter is, in this play as elsewhere, refusing to pin down a character so as to allow him to be viewed in a more symbolic, universal way. In *No Man's Land* Pinter offers little traditional exposition except to set the scene and to allow the characters to divulge information about themselves which may or may not be true. What he has avoided is the insistent use of exposition to pin down the facts about character and incident which leave the audience in no doubt as to the theme or, simply, the story-line. Pinter, ironically, might indeed be said to be for once speaking through the mouth of one of his characters on this subject:

> Experience is a paltry thing. Eveyone has it and will tell his tale of it. I leave experience to psychological interpreters, the wetdream world. I myself can do any graph of experience you wish, to suit your taste or mine. Child's play. The present will not be distorted.   (p. 20)

The very terms in which Spooner invites Hirst to hold forth concerning his past life suggests, mockingly, that the whole venture is suspect:

Tell me more with all the authority and brilliance you can muster, about the socio-politico-economic structure of the environment in which you attained to the age of reason.   (p. 30)

Spooner's further comment places the emphasis on essence as opposed to superficial particularities – and this in turn may be said to reflect Pinter's concern with poetic, universal truths about the human condition rather than with mere factual details about people:

Tell me then about your wife. . . . I begin to wonder whether truly accurate and therefore essentially poetic definition means anything to you at all. I begin to wonder whether you do in fact truly remember her. . . . Her eyes, I take it, were hazel?   (pp. 30–1)

I feel Pinter is reacting strongly against the way that characters in rep plays present factual information about themselves. He mistrusts what is often taken for sincerity or a 'true' confession of past actions or motives. A good example of the 'confession speech' in a typical fifties rep play is provided by a comedy Pinter acted in called *Ring for Catty* (Cargill and Beale). Madge's boyfriend is dying of consumption in a servicemen's convalescent home, and she explains her motives for leaving him to a patient who has recently befriended him:

GRAY. Madge. Were you in love with Len?

MADGE. I honestly can't say now. We grew up together, went to school together, did everything together, it's natural to be fond of him. I always will be, but I don't think it was love, not now. It might have become love, but what chance did we have? I was only eighteen when he came in here. I said I'd marry him, I know, because I could have done. I could easily have spent the rest of my life with him if this hadn't happened – his being ill, I mean. We could have been very happy, and I think we would have grown to love each other deeply. But during these last two years that Len has been lying in here he's been living on a memory. But it hasn't really been hard for him. All he's had is my photo, this record and a picture in his mind of what things were like two years ago. His world has stopped, but mine has

gone on and I've had to go on with it. For me things have
changed – I've changed – and Len is left behind. There's
time and space between us now, Don, between my world
of reality and his world of memory. I've tried to get back to
him, but I can't. If he'd been with me that night at the
pictures I wouldn't have seen that man, not if I'd looked at
him for ten minutes. Do you understand, Don?

GRAY.   Those were the words you'd planned to say to him,
weren't they?[7]

The speech has, it is assumed, been prepared, yet the audience is still
expected to accept its sincerity and truthfulness, especially as it is the
only extended piece of exposition relating to the nature of the
relationship the hero of the play has depended on as the reason to
live. As part of a sentimental drama the speech is of course quite
acceptable, but as such it lacks the natural, unstudied effect
inherent in actual speech – even after taking into account the
'planned' nature of the young woman's words. Moreover, as so often
in the conventional rep play, all that the playwright wishes to
convey is conveyed through the words, and little if anything
between or under the words. In short, there is no subtext. For
Pinter, however, 'below the word spoken is the thing known and
unspoken'.[8] The typical fifties play was replete with sentiments
expressed in carefully phrased monologues such as the above, with
the understanding that if a character was not being sincere there
would be enough indications to prevent ambiguity. Pinter, on the
other hand, exploits to the full the ambiguities and deceits inherent
in spoken language and achieves his own kind of realistic effect. In
the quoted passage from *Ring for Catty* – which may serve as an
example of well-made-play exposition – the sentimental tone and
somewhat studied repetitions create an artificial effect. The passage
is also a fairly obvious piece of contrived exposition, in so far as the
speaker had no real need to tell a man to whom she had just
introduced herself a romantic autobiography. The purpose of
introducing such speeches is to put the audience in possession of the
necessary information without which the subsequent action of the
play would not be understood. If there was to be contradiction or
doubt in a play it was to exist, temporarily, in the minds of the
characters and be resolved by the end of the play. But, as previously
stated, for Pinter the principle of uncertainty is built much more
deeply into the fabric of the play, and any 'irritable reaching after

fact and reason' the audience may indulge in is resisted by his pursuit of what Keats termed 'Negative Capability . . . when a man is capable of being in uncertainties, mysteries, doubts'. For Nigel Dennis, Bernard Levin, Clive James and others this is a form of treachery, of teasing the audience to no purpose. On the contrary, Pinter argues,

> a character who can present no convincing argument or information as to his past experience, his present behaviour or his aspirations, nor give a comprehensive analysis of his motives is as legitimate and as worthy of attention as one who, alarmingly, can do all these things. The more acute the experience, the less articulate its expression . . . so often, below the word spoken, is the thing known and unspoken. My characters tell me so much and no more, with reference to their experience, their aspirations, their motives, their history. Between my lack of biographical data about them and the ambiguity of what they say lies a territory which is not only worthy of exploration but which is compulsory to explore . . . most of the time we're inexpressive, giving little away, unreliable, elusive, evasive, obstructive, unwilling. But it's out of these attributes that a language arises. A language when under what is said another thing is being said. [9]

There is one example, however, of a speech in a Pinter play which seems to have a straightforward expository significance: Aston's concluding Act II monologue in *The Caretaker* (though Pinter characteristically suggests that it is not necessary to conclude that everything that Aston says about his experience in the mental hospital is true). To John Elsom the speech is reminiscent of the confessional curtain speech of the typical rep play: 'The soliloquy confessions of drawing room dramas became such speeches as the hesitant reminiscence of Aston in *The Caretaker* – at the end of Act II – the traditional place for curtain confessions.' [10] Pinter had in effect allowed a character to muse aloud in almost the same manner as a Shakespearian character soliloquising. Aston's extended version of the events that have brought him to his present position of ineffectiveness is in a sense addressed to the audience rather than to another character on stage. The spotlighting-effect helps this illusion. However, it is possible to see Aston's self-revelation as directly and inevitably related to the very kernel of his personality. A. E. Quigley has succinctly pointed out how Aston's problem has been, and remains, a verbal one. Before the mental-hospital experience Aston 'talked too much'; his problem after the electric-shock treatment is not solved but further complicated – verbal communication becomes even more difficult:

> Aston has a peculiar impact on the flow of dialogue because . . . he is not fully in touch with the rules. He does not promote or extend conversations because he does not rapidly grasp 'what is being done with the words'. His speed of thought is slow, and so is his ability to perceive the movement of a conversation. Because of this, he himself is not extensively involved in *or revealed in* dialogue. To Aston then, the need to get closely involved in a relationship requires a long, elaborate self-revelatory speech of this sort. It is not inconsistent with his previous verbal behaviour though it may be different from it. This speech has been foreshadowed in his earlier disjunctive statements about the drink of Guinness and the woman asking to see his body.[11]

In the same play Aston's brother Mick uses long monologue-style speeches for purposes other than the traditional one of giving information or forwarding the plot. He utilises language as a means of taunting attack on the intruding figure of Davies; he is at the same time asserting his own authority and displaying for Davies's 'benefit' a dazzling and confusing verbal dexterity. Three early speeches stand out as worthy of mention here: first, the absurd flight of fancies beginning 'You remind me of my uncle's brother' (p. 40); secondly, the speech about the 'bloke' from Shoreditch which incorporates meticulous references to London bus routes (p. 41); and, thirdly, the mock business arrangement Mick proposes to Davies as prospective tenant (pp. 44–5). Now, with regard to the first speech, the question of whether Mick's uncle's brother exists, is his father or, more incredibly, is as he describes him is not of moment; what is is Mick's technique of bewildering and disorienting the tramp by conjuring up a character so unlike Davies – athletic, sexually attractive, organised, equipped with the necessary papers ('Never without his passport') – and then brazenly calling him the 'spitting image' of Davies. Again, it does not matter whether the story of the bloke he knew in Shoreditch who had a pitch in Finsbury Park and was brought up in Putney is true or not. As Quigley has further remarked,

> Though the kind of jargon Mick resorts to gives us some indication of his own self-image, it would not be helpful to devote

a great deal of time to disentangle his past or his career from this hotchpotch of words, we would clearly be missing the activity in which he is engaged.[12]

It is quite clearly the pressing-home of the verbal assault that we admire, as Mick parades his topographical expertise – his effortless mastery of London's transport system – to point up Davies's rootlessness and bewildered 'stranger' status. Similarly, in the third tirade, it is irrelevant to speculate on how much Mick is 'putting on' the respectable property-owner image – the man with his own solicitor and a brother who's a number-one decorator (!): he plays the role, however simulated, with gusto and conviction and completes the demoralisation of Davies.

Turning now to consider endings, the resolution of the action, the final scenes of some of the rep plays in relation to Pinter, we note Pinter's insistence on the usefulness of the proscenium-arch curtain: 'I write curtain lines for that reason.' This comment need not be taken too literally, since it may be seen to relate rather to his sense of shape and structure, to his instinctive feeling for where to end his plays. It is true, none the less, that in many of the rep plays a strong curtain line that elicits applause or provides the final ironic or melodramatic twist is often considered very important. The 'curtain ending' at its melodramatic extreme is, in fact, not far short of Gothic or Victorian extravagance. An example might be the final curtain of Agatha Christie's *Witness for the Prosecution*, in which Pinter played Mayhew, the defending counsel, in 1955. This most popular thriller ends with twist and counter-twist to the plot. Leonard Vole's charm and his faithful wife Romaine's maniacal vindictiveness are both seen to be fabrications:

ROMAINE. Is – this – true? Is she your girl, Leonard?

LEONARD. Yes, she is.

ROMAINE. After all I've done for you ... What can she do for you that can compare with that?

LEONARD. She's 15 years younger than you are. I've got the money. I've been acquitted, and I can't be tried again, so don't go shooting off your mouth, or you'll just get yourself hanged as an accessory after the fact.

He turns to THE GIRL *and embraces her.*
ROMAINE *picks up the knife from the table.*

ROMAINE. No that will not happen. I shall not be tried as an accessory after the fact. I shall not be tried for perjury. I shall be tried for murder (*she stabs him in the back*) – the murder of the only man I ever loved.

(LEONARD *drops.* THE GIRL *screams.* MAYHEW *bends over* LEONARD, *feels his pulse and shakes his head. She looks up at* THE JUDGES'*s seat.*) Guilty, my lord.

CURTAIN [13]

This kind of sensational tableau, reminiscent of Grand Guignol, is not, of course, present in the Pinter canon. But he often uses his own kind of dramatic image to end a play. *The Dumb Waiter* and *The Room* are instances of Pinter's early tendency to place strong climaxes at the end of his plays: *The Dumb Waiter* ends with a surprise murder – an ironic final 'twist' to the plot – about to be committed, or apparently so, with the two gunmen frozen for the first time in direct confrontation with one another. *The Room* perhaps comes closest to the violence of the passage quoted above: Bert, the quiet but potentially aggressive tenant of the room, suddenly and violently kills the blind negro intruder and thus strangely brings about his wife's blindness at the final curtain. It should at once be pointed out how quickly Pinter learned to avoid such overtly violent endings. In the interview with *New Theatre Magazine* he was asked, 'Do you know soon after you have begun a play where it is likely to stop?' His answer is rooted in his realisation of the power of the characters as it were to govern the plot:

> At the end of *The Caretaker*, there are two people alone in a room, and one of them must go in such a way as to produce a sense of complete separation and finality. I thought originally that the play must end with the violent death of one at the hands of the other. But then I realised, when I got to the point, that the characters as they had grown could never act in this way. [14]

What does end *The Caretaker* is a long silence after Davies's broken pleas to be allowed to stay in the brothers' flat. Martin Esslin has recognised the suitability of this ending: 'the whole course of the play has organically and inevitably led up to it'. [15] The characters fall silent not because they find themselves unable to speak but because they recognise that all they can usefully say has already been said. Thus it can be seen how Pinter more subtly confines the aggression and violence in his plays to the language, and uses an image, a 'tableau', to create the 'curtain'. *The Homecoming* has its own final tableau: an apparently dead man lying prostrate on the carpet together with a snivelling old man kneeling at the feet of a woman who has meaningfully taken over his chair as head of the household; *Old Times* ends with the symbolic dumb-show of the play's male figure wavering in despair between the beds of the two women who have become so distant from him in the course of the play. Pinter's view of last-act 'messages' is clearly stated early in a speech he gave at the National Student Drama Festival in Bristol, 1962:

A play is not an essay, nor should a playwright under any exhortation damage the consistency of his characters by injecting a remedy or apology for their actions into the last act, simply because we have been brought up to expect, rain or sunshine, the last act 'resolution'. To supply an explicit moral tag to an evolving and compulsive dramatic image seems to be facile, impertinent and dishonest. Where this takes place it is not theatre but a crossword puzzle. The audience holds the paper. The play fills in the blanks. Everyone's happy. [16]

A typical resolution of many a traditional comedy is a marriage or the restoration of marital harmony. The message usually comes across loud and clear in the final act that marriage is a status to be clung to despite all indications to the contrary – the main one being the incompatibility of the marital partners! In his repertory experience Pinter was involved in many plays where the playwright's message was contrived to the extent of spoiling the natural developments of characterisation. Dennis Cannan's comedy *You and Your Wife*, in which Pinter had a leading role whilst at Colchester, is worthy of consideration here. The last two acts are in effect an extended 'explicit moral tag' in a double sense: the dialogue and the stage action underline the message that marital fidelity is preferable to the enticements of adultery. Two married couples who are involved in 'triangular' relationships with each other are detained in the house of one couple by two ingenious burglars. Rather incredibly, there then follows a discussion, which at times resembles a sociologists' symposium, on marriage and adultery and the ethical and psychological problems inherent in each. The intellectual or at least quasi-intellectual tenor of the conversation may be appropriate for one of the foursome – a man with literary and philosophical inclinations – but is totally foreign to the personalities of the three others, who are distinctly non-academic types! The fact that the couples are brought together by well reasoned, progressively developed logical argument is perhaps more disturbing – in terms of dramatic credibility – than the four characters' acceptance of their farcical situation: eventually, through being each tied to a leg of the same table, they are made somewhat painfully aware of the inescapability of the bonds of marriage! The married couple in *The Lover* have 'triangular' relationships, but these are imaginary, involving merely the two of them. Richard and Sarah play 'relationship' or 'lover' games with one another, and, after attempting at one stage to dispense with their game of pretending to be lovers, as distinct from spouses, find themselves unable to exist except in their fantasy roles. Interestingly, at this point the play ends with a table in full centre-stage focus. The two characters attempt first to evade one another by means of the table, but eventually succumb to seduction kneeling in front of it. Pinter's method of summing up the relationship in this final scene of a one-act play depends on the implicit and ironic rather than the explicit and moralistic:

> *She retreats towards the table, eventually ending behind it.*

> RICHARD. Come on don't be a spoilsport. Your husband won't mind if you give me a light. You look a little pale. Why are you so pale? A lovely girl like you?

> *He begins to move slowly closer to the table*

> You can't get out, darling. You're trapped.

> *They face each other from opposite ends of the table*

> SARAH. I'm trapped. . . . What will my husband say?

> *She looks at him, bends and begins to crawl under the table towards him. She emerges from under the table and kneels at his feet, looking up. . . .*

Would you like me to change? Would you like me to change
my clothes? . . .

RICHARD. Yes. . . . Change. . . . Change. . . . Change   your
clothes . . . . you lovely whore.

They are still, kneeling, she leaning over him.

THE END   (pp. 194–6)

It is useful, here, to compare the situation at the end of *The Lover*
with an end-of-act sequence from a comedy that may consciously or
unconsciously have influenced Pinter in several ways. The play
concerned is *Late Love* by Rosemary Casey. Pinter played the second
male lead in Huddersfield in 1954, and was in the Colchester
production the following summer. His observation 'under what is
said, another thing is being said' is relevant here. In *Late Love* the
main theme is the pretence indulged in by a mother (Mrs Colby)
and son (Graham Colby). Graham is a writer who leads a
determinedly sheltered ascetic existence, claiming to be under the
restraining influence of a domineering mother, who in fact adopts
this role for her own amusement, drinking gin under the guise of
lemonade and listening to the radio in secret. Graham in reality is in
general control of his mother, or imagines he is. At the end of the first
act he, in his adopted role of mother-dominated grown-up child,
attempts to woo the open, friendly Constance, a painter who is
visiting the Colby household. In this scene, as at the end of *The Lover*,
emphasis is placed on the lighting of a cigarette as a symbolic
introduction to intimacy; and, in addition to the role-playing of
mother and son, there is an emphasis on what is implied rather than
what is said:

GRAHAM. Would you like a cigarette now?
CONSTANCE. Certainly not! Your mother might come in at any
     moment!
GRAHAM. She probably will! . . .
CONSTANCE. I don't actually want a cigarette at this minute!
GRAHAM. You would be doing me a favour if you took one! (*He
     says this with such firmness that* CONSTANCE *smiles.*)
CONSTANCE. Then I shall of course. (*Takes out cigarette case and box of
     matches.*)
GRAHAM. Let me light it for you.

MRS COLBY *enters*.

MRS COLBY. Graham! What are you doing?!
CONSTANCE. He's lighting my cigarette!

He is lighting it as

THE CURTAIN FALLS [17]

Rosemary Casey's act-ending is, of course, more contrived than Pinter's: the on-cue entrance of the third character rounds off everything so conveniently! Yet the agreed adoption of a role-playing game by two characters, the symbolic use of a prop and the importance of what is implied underneath what is said are features common to both playwrights.

In a previously quoted extract from the Richard Findlater interview Pinter mentions that his experience as an actor had given him 'a pretty good notion . . . of what would shut an audience up'. The detective play or whodunnit, through use of dramatic tension and suspense, provide one obvious example of this kind of audience manipulation. And crucial to this type of effect is the way the playwright handles the gradual revelations of past events or of the true state of affairs in the present. This revelation of the past has been a traditional theme amongst the writers of the well-made play – the master being Henrik Ibsen – and it has become an essential formula for the writers of detective plays, such as Agatha Christie, and the authors of romantic dramas or thrillers, such as Daphne du Maurier: nearly always there is doubt or mystery surrounding a death or murder which is eventually removed when the facts about events and characters are finally ascertained. This often involves a detailed examination of different characters' views of what may or may not have happened as the 'suspects' in a murder play go over the same ground under questioning. In Agatha Christie's *Witness for the Prosecution*, for example, a man and his wife give conflicting accounts of the circumstances surrounding the murder of which he is accused. One may compare with this the element of mystery and suspense in *Old Times*: here, as in other Pinter plays, the existence of a number of different versions of particular events owes something to the detective play. *Old Times* gains much of its own kind of suspense or tension from the use of cross-references to past incidents: Deeley and Anna have their own versions of the Westbourne Grove party and the cinema visit to see *Odd Man Out*, and at one point in Act I Anna describes in fine detail the despairing movements of Deeley at the end of the play. Finding out what actually happened in the past and exactly what sort of relationships exist between the characters provides the dramatic impetus of *Old Times*, even if there are no precise answers. It is here, of course, that we touch upon a fundamental issue for Pinter: the desire to remove himself from the position of the omniscient author. The search for the final truth about a character is likely to be an unfulfilled one. For Pinter this is as true of life as it is of his drama:

> The desire for verification on the part of all of us, with regard to our own experience and the experience of others, is understandable but cannot always be satisfied. I suggest there can be no hard distinctions between what is real and what is unreal, nor between what is true and what is false.[18]

Of course, the haunting, poetic quality of the Pinter play gives it a quite different atmosphere from the typical thriller, such as *Witness for the Prosecution*, or a more literary work, such as *Rebecca*; yet in all three plays the ascertaining of the truth about the past, and the tensions produced by the eternal-triangle theme are of prime dramatic significance. *Rebecca*, like *Old Times*, involves much dialogue relating to the characters' past lives and is broken up by extended stories which in their turn relate to the past or plausibly seem to do so. In *Rebecca* the stories are mostly concerned with the character of the first Mrs de Winter – the Rebecca of the title – and her relationship with her husband, in addition to the circumstances surrounding her mysterious death. In *Old Times* the stories relate to the characters' past and vary in levels of apparent seriousness from descriptions of parties or visits to the cinema to the retelling of incidents of a more private, sexual nature. Whether the stories are true or not is of only relative importance in Pinter's play; in the thriller the truth of a 'story' related to a crime or possible murder is, of course, of crucial importance. When Maxim de Winter tells his version of how his first wife apparently met her death, it is primarily a case of imparting vital information to the audience, as well as a beginning to his coming to terms with the past. In Pinter's *Old Times*, when Deeley tells his story of his visit to the film *Odd Man Out* or to the party at Westbourne Grove the playwright does not intend to give information which may logically lead on to the play's dénouement in a linear sequence of cause and effect. The various versions of the party and the cinema visit are essentially counters in a competitive game played by Deeley and Anna, mainly over their relationship with Kate. Truth for Pinter and his characters is indeed subject to negotiation, a variable, intangible thing. Tension in a detective play or thriller often arises from a desire on the audience's part to know the truth of the matter in a murder story; in a Pinter play, tension often arises from a struggle for mastery between characters who may or may not be telling the truth about their past.

Closely related to this last point is the question of true or false evidence. In a whodunnit the audience is often presented with a lie or purposefully false information, and naturally enough this usually emanates from the guilty party. (In *Witness for the Prosecution* both innocent and guilty parties tell falsehoods for different motives.) In Pinter's plays, as has been argued, we are often uncertain of the truth or falsehood of a character's words, often as a result of role-playing, deliberate self-contradiction, plain hostility or mere vagueness on the part of the character. A minor example of this point is Briggs's seemingly gratuitous, almost surreal account of his first meeting with Foster in *No Man's Land*. He tells Spooner his tale of directing his new-found friend through the maze of one-way streets in London's West End. The story opens and closes with the same remark: 'I should tell you he'll deny this account. His story will be different.' In a detective play a character's assertion that another will give a different version of events usually makes the content of what is said of extreme importance: one version is presumably a true one and the other false. The question of whether the character is telling the truth, however, does not here concern Pinter, and Briggs, with his deliberate acknowledgement that there is more than one version of the story, in a sense reflects his creator's own attitude to the verifiability of past events. On one level the speech is in the best traditions of the music-hall comic monologue, especially in the seemingly never-ending list of minutiae – at first plausible, then increasingly more outrageous and surreal. On another level it is an example of language used as a weapon to confuse and psychologically to disorient the imprisoned guest, whom Briggs has previously treated with undisguised contempt:

> I told him his best bet, if he really wanted to get to Bolsover street, was to take the first left, first right, second right, third on the left, keep his eye open for a hardware shop . . . reverse into the

underground car park, change gear, go straight on, and he'll find himself in Bolsover street with no trouble at all. . . . I told him I knew one or two people who'd been wandering up and down Bolsover street for years. They'd wasted their bloody youth there. . . . Normally I wouldn't give a fuck.   (pp. 62–3)

It is, then, the role-playing indulged in by the speaker as cynical comic raconteur, and his underlying contemptuous hostility directed at his captive audience, Spooner, which is important in the speech. On a more general level the speech may be regarded as a partly comic, partly serious metaphor for the play's thematic concern with the aimlessness of existence, the mental labyrinths formed by insecurity and unsureness of identity and the past.

The earlier play *The Collection* is based on conflicting stories about a possible case of seduction, which is never finally revealed as either truth or fabrication. Ronald Hayman succinctly points out Pinter's prime intentions in writing this original kind of mystery play (in which a man believes that his wife has slept with another man when they were both staying at an hotel in Leeds): 'the action succeeds in showing that what "really" happened in Leeds hardly matters at all. What matters is the insecurities that the characters have about themselves and about each other.'[19]

Not all of Pinter's characters are so complex or mystifying when it comes to the subject of truth-telling, but even his apparently most simple-minded and sincere character, Aston in *The Caretaker*, need not be taken completely at face value. Pinter himself commented on Aston's soliloquy at the end of Act II, with its powerful recounting of experiences in a mental hospital,

My purpose was to let him go on talking until he was finished and then . . . bring the curtain down. I had no axe to grind there. And the one thing that people have missed is that it isn't necessary to conclude that everything Aston says about his experiences in the mental hospital is true.[20]

A special kind of tension and dramatic excitement was often produced by the interrogation scenes in the typical detective plays which formed such a large part of the repertory companies' staple material. These scenes might easily have been noted by Pinter the actor as being capable of shutting an audience up. Pinter's own variations on this theme may be usefully studied at this point.

The detectives and inspectors that Pinter often successfully
played in the many whodunnits and thrillers of his repertory career
have been seen by many critics (including John Elsom and Michael
Billington[21]) as source material for the inquisitional Goldberg and
McCann in *The Birthday Party*. Other interrogators in Pinter's plays,
such as Lenny in *The Homecoming*, Mick in *The Caretaker* and Foster
and Briggs in *No Man's Land*, may seem less like theatrical
descendants of police inspectors, but they do in their own individual
and indirect way question people seemingly at their mercy, though
unlike the whodunnit inspectors they do not appear to have fact-
finding as their main motive for interrogation. Lenny is insidious
and sardonic in the extreme when taunting either Teddy or his wife;
Mick is savagely ironic in tormenting Davies with questions about
his immediate past; and Foster and Briggs are by turns vulgarly
abusive and dismissively facetious in their questioning of their
master's intrusive guest, Spooner. They are truly a far cry from the
straightforward and morally upright police sergeant or inspector,
such as Agatha Christie's Inspector Colquhoun in *The Hollow*, or the
dogged, modest and unassuming Detective Constable in Jack
Popplewell's *The Vanity Case*. But Pinter as David Baron often
managed to transform or at least colour these roles with his own
macabre, sardonic or suave style, as has already been noted.
Indeed, Pinter even managed to make the apparently dry role of the
police investigator in *The Vanity Case* into a successful study injected
with humour.[22] Previously quoted notices of Pinter's successes as
inspectors and detectives refer to his playing 'a suave member of the
CID', an 'insidious' detective, an 'almost too charming detective
sergeant', and a plain-clothes 'dick' with 'half-ingratiating, half-
cynical smile'. It is interesting to note here 'DM's' review in the
Gloucestershire Echo for 19 September 1960 of Pinter's performance as
Goldberg: 'Mr Pinter plays the slick, insinuating stranger with
absolute conviction, masking his fearsome and almost dispassionate
cruelty with a svelte charm which makes it all the more menacing.'
The interrogators of Pinter's own plays are often noted for
possessing a suave manner or a cynical or ingratiating tone of
address, and in their different ways may be termed 'insidious'. But
the important distinction to be made between the repertory
inspectors and Pinter's interrogators – apart from their official and
unofficial roles as inquisitors – is that, whereas the characters David
Baron often played had as their prime occupational role the finding-
out of factual truths about people, the characters created by Pinter

the playwright are more concerned with asserting their own dominance over the people they taunt rather than interrogate.

The standard detective play is, then, to be traced as a possible source for the inquisitions carried out by several of Pinter's characters in the plays mentioned. There usually is, however, no real attempt on behalf of the Pinter 'detective' to unearth facts from the victim of the interrogation. Stanley Webber in *The Birthday Party* is subjected to a barrage of questions part comic, part menacing in an attempt to extract a confession of guilt with regard to an unmentioned crime, arguably the existential crime of failure:

GOLDBERG. Webber you're a fake. . . . When did you last wash up a cup?

STANLEY. The Christmas before last.

GOLDBERG. Where?

STANLEY. Lyons Corner House.

GOLDBERG. Which one?

STANLEY. Marble Arch.

GOLDBERG. Where was your wife?

STANLEY. In –

GOLDBERG. Answer.

STANLEY (*turning, crouched*). What wife?

GOLDBERG. What have you done with your wife?

MCCANN. He's killed his wife.

GOLDBERG. Why did you kill your wife?

STANLEY (*sitting, his back to the audience*). What wife?

MCCANN. How did he kill her?

GOLDBERG. How did you kill her?

MCCANN. You throttled her.

GOLDBERG. With arsenic.

MCCANN. There's your man!   (p. 59)

If the audience are in any way beginning to feel that at last Stanley's interrogators are getting down to a recognisable murder investigation, they are of course instantly undeceived; Goldberg as before switches his line of frenzied inquiry, admitting the strong possibility that Stanley had never married, and soon flies off into bogus philosophical questions and sundry irrelevant taunts concerning Irish history and cricketing-scandals, and plain verbal abuse.

Pinter makes some farcical use of the interrogation scene in his early and previously discarded play *The Hothouse*. Act 1 ends with the truly innocent 'sacrificial' Lamb being grilled by the cynical bureaucratic officials Gibbs and Miss Cutts. The stichomythia effect of their questioning and the use of electrode-based shock treatment may be seen as material to be compared and contrasted with the Goldberg and McCann interrogation scene and the unelicited confessions of Aston, which involve a more serious account of electric therapy:

> LAMB *jolts rigid, his hands to his earphones, he is propelled from the chair, falls, stands, falls, rolls, clutching his earphones, crawls under the table . . . silence . . . .*

CUTTS. Are you virgo intacta?
LAMB. What?
CUTTS. Are you virgo intacta?
LAMB. Oh, I say, that's rather embarrassing. I mean, in front of a lady –
CUTTS. Are you virgo intacta?
LAMB. Yes, I am, actually. I'll make no secret of it.
CUTTS. Have you always been virgo intacta?
LAMB. Oh yes, always. Always.
CUTTS. From the word go?
LAMB. Go? Oh yes. From the word go.
GIBBS. What is the law of the Wolf Cub Pack?   (pp. 73–4)

But closer to the usual format of police questioning is Pinter's parody of the idea that the policeman/detective is cleverer than the criminal. The play ends with the bland and ludicrously short-sighted interview between the obviously homicidal Gibbs and his superior:

GIBBS. The whole staff was slaughtered, sir.
LOBB. The whole staff?
GIBBS. With one exception, of course.
LOBB. Who was that?
GIBBS. Me, Sir.
LOBB. Oh yes, of course. (*Pause.*) The whole staff, eh? A massacre, in fact?
GIBBS. Exactly.
LOBB. Most distressing. (*Pause.*) How did they ... how did they do it?

GIBBS. Various means, Sir. Mr Roote and Miss Cutts were
  stabbed in their bed. Lush –
LOBB. Excuse me, did you say bed, or beds?
GIBBS. Bed, Sir.
LOBB. Oh, really? Yes go on.
GIBBS. Lush, Hogg, Beck, Budd, Tuck, Dodds, Tate and Pett, Sir,
  were hanged and strangled, variously.
LOBB. I see. Well, I can see there's going to be a lot of questions
  asked about this, Gibbs. (pp. 148–50)

Thus, from Roote through to Pett, Pinter delighted in producing in
encapsulated satiric form his own version of *Ten Little Niggers!*

In the thrillers and occasional comedies and farces in which he
played, many examples of effective lighting- and sound-effects –
blackouts, gunshots, mysterious lights or atmospheric noises off –
would also have suggested to Pinter ways of shutting an audience
up. In *Waiting for Gillian*, a thriller written by Ronald Millar and
Nigel Balchin, there is a theatrically effective moment in the drama
when a car's headlamps are seen arcing round the blacked-out room
of a man whose wife is under suspicion of being the hit-and-run
driver of the car in question. Here the lighting-effect has symbolic
significance: it is as if the light were searching out the guilty party,
the Gillian of the title. In Pinter's *The Birthday Party* the guilty
person being searched out by a light in a blacked-out room is of
course, Stanley Webber, dazzled in the glare from the torch of his
mysterious interrogator, McCann. In *Reluctant Heroes*, a popular
Whitehall farce of the fifties, an Army Sergeant (the role played by
Pinter) ends the first scene by directing a tirade at his raw National
Service recruits before peremptorily switching off the barrack-room
lights on exiting: end of scene; no more talking! A similar though
subtler form of aggression occurs in *No Man's Land* when Foster
completes his tactic of putting down Spooner by literally
'blacking him out', switching off the lights and thereby ending the
act:

(FOSTER *walks about the room, stops at the door.*) Listen. You know
what it's like when you're in a room with the light on and then
suddenly the light goes out? I'll show you. It's like this. (*He turns
the light out.*)

BLACKOUT   (p. 53)

There is both menace and humour in Foster's mocking 'obliter-ation' of his victim, and perhaps by extension in the playwright's slightly teasing way of drawing attention to his own decision to end the act there.

Gunshots or screams penetrating a silent blackout are common in the thrillers of the period in question. There are examples of this simple theatrical device in Agatha Christie whodunnits such as *Spider's Web* and *Peril at End House*, but perhaps most memorably in Jack Popplewell's *Dead on Nine*, in which shots are fired in a cliff-top house whilst outside the sounds of a tempest accompany the murder. Storms appropriately formed the 'atmospheric' background for many a murder in the classic thriller or whodunnit, *The Hollow* being a famous example. Pinter has usually been subtler in his use of sound-effects during blackouts. Perhaps his most successful effect is the electrolux (vacuum cleaner) used by Mick in *The Caretaker*. Its noise is used to terrify the intruding Davies during a blackout, simply and neatly effected by Mick's using the light-bulb socket as source of power for the cleaner. The blackout scene in *The Birthday Party* has already been referred to. The scene further gains in effectiveness from the sounds of Stanley's hysterical giggling and the staccato beating of his toy drum as he cracks under the pressure exerted by his persecutors. Another play in which Pinter acted that may have remained in his mind to influence the blackout scenes in *The Birthday Party* and *The Caretaker* is R. F. Delderfield's war comedy *Worm's Eye View*. The necessity for observing a war-time blackout is the key to the comic climax at the end of Act II. In this scene a prolonged attempt is made to remove the ceiling light-bulb by a character climbing onto a table centre-stage whilst an impromptu party chaotically begins following the discovery of a clandestine pair of young lovers in a Northern seaside billet. The effect of all this climactic action is very different, of course, from the atmosphere of menace and terror with which the party at Meg's South-coast boarding-house in *The Birthday Party* reaches its conclusion, as Stanley backs away from the spreadeagled Lulu with his own macabre party game exposed. Yet, as in other instances where the repertory play may have influenced the plays of Harold Pinter, it must be carefully borne in mind that rarely does Pinter simply borrow an effect or a convention: rather, he transforms it into something in very much his own style.

Gunshots, screams and atmospheric noises generally – whether in or out of a blackout – are all but absent from Pinter's plays. The closest he gets to atmospheric noises off – his equivalent of the moaning wind or melodramatic storm without – are the amplified sighs, keenings and laughter that occasionally act as auditory links between scenes in the eerie government-run rest-home that provides the setting of *The Hothouse*. Although there is a naturalistic basis for these sound-effects – the tape-recordings of hysterical mental patients – in the theatre the effects have an eerie, surreal quality more suitable to a more poetic kind of drama. A similar kind of surreal effect is achieved in Anouilh's *Point of Departure*, in which high-frequency humming and drum noises are used as quasi-musical accompaniment to the tragedy. It was as Orpheus in this play early in 1955 that 'David Baron' achieved one of his major successes. The sound-effect more usually associated with Pinter the playwright is the quieter, more mundane one of a door shutting. Yet, as in several instances in *The Caretaker*, including the opening sequence, the sound of a door shutting off stage can be as effective in building up tension as a gunshot in a thriller. The effect Pinter achieves thereby is of course more subtle than sensational! 'Whenever I write for the stage, I merely see the stage I've been used to. . . . I always think of the normal picture frame stage which I used as an actor.'[23]

Pinter here acknowledges the importance for him of the traditional proscenium-arch stage, with the audience looking through the fourth wall, and looking (in most rep plays) at a single set for the whole evening. The kind of focus and discipline provided by this limited and enclosed acting-area leads directly to Pinter's distinctive use of the room. Many critics have written perceptively on this important element in Pinter's work. Peter Hall, for example, notes that 'All Pinter's work relates to a confined space where people confront each other in often very ugly terms.'[24] Arthur Ganz in *Twentieth Century Views: Pinter* comments, 'The room becomes for Pinter a way of blocking out the diffuse claims of the external world and concentrating on the central facts of existence as he conceives of them.'[25] Most pertinently reference might be made to Katharine Worth's view of the relevance of the proscenium-arch stage to Pinter's art: 'Secrecy is Pinter's great subject, his most compelling reasons for always using the proscenium, the closed, framed stage where the characters can be shut up and spied upon.'[26]

Early in his career as a playwright Pinter explained as follows his concern with the individual, private worlds of people rather than wider sociological and political issues:

Before you manage to adjust yourself to living alone in your
room . . . you are not terribly fit and equipped to go out and fight
battles . . . which are fought mostly in abstractions in the outside
world.[27]

This kind of focus on the room as a symbolic battle-ground or
hiding-place, or simply an enclosed area in which people's in-
nermost feelings are revealed, is rarely if ever achieved in the typical
rep play Pinter acted in in the fifties. Pinter's characters may at
times be seen as being metaphorically marooned from the outside
world in their rooms; in the occasional thriller and more rarely in
comedy there is presented a situation where characters are literally
marooned or cut off from the outside world. In *The Birthday Party*, for
example, Stanley Webber is very much an isolated, marooned
figure in his seaside digs; there is for him no escape from his fate,
symbolised best perhaps by the image of him cowering, back to the
wall, in his hysterical attempt to escape from the clutches of his
persecutors, Goldberg and McCann. Other Pinter characters, such
as Aston in *The Caretaker* and Hirst in *No Man's Land*, seem in their
different ways divorced or isolated from the outside world in their
own living-space and feel threatened when that space is intruded
upon by someone who, although an invited guest, makes claims for
territorial possession. The idea of 'shutting up' characters in a
confined setting has obvious dramatic possibilities, and in the rep
plays a number of examples of such confinement occur, but without
the poetic or symbolic effects Pinter achieves. In *Ten Little Niggers*
ten characters, including a murderer, are literally temporarily
marooned on an island. In a comedy called *Here We Come Gathering*
which Pinter experienced early in his career as a rep actor, the
action takes place in a newly-weds' cottage surrounded by a mill-
stream whose only bridge collapses, leaving the characters marooned and causing some of them to readjust the nature of their
relationships. The tensions and frictions caused by being cut off from
the outside world in a newly acquired remote cottage, without food
and furniture, cause a meek husband and a dominated, recently
married son to rebel against their oppressive wife/mother. But,
whereas both Agatha Christie and the comedy writers Philip King
and Anthony Armstrong contrive to get their characters into the
isolated setting, removing them from their accustomed environment, Pinter usually focuses from the beginning, through the room,
on loners whose world it represents.

Before examination of further examples of the single set as it appeared in fifties rep plays it is worth noting that Pinter showed an interest in the theme of the room in the early years of his English acting-career. 'The Examination', a short story, was written in 1955 following a barren year as a mainly unemployed actor, no doubt living alone in digs. Pinter writes in a formal style, reminiscent of some of Beckett's prose, which he has acknowledged as influential; the subject concerns the scarcely perceptible psychological struggle for the ownership of a room between the first-person narrator and Kullus. The narrator allows Kullus to enter his room for the purpose of taking an examination or simply for 'talks'; eventually, however, by allowing Kullus intervals or breaks in the 'examination', the host is dominated by the silences the intruder imposes, and in effect Kullus gains the room. The subtle usurpation of his room leaves the narrator alarmed, confounded and subservient. The room for Pinter thus early on took on a symbolic significance, as private territory which might be threatened from a hostile world outside. Pinter must have experienced a great many actors' lodgings from his early days with Anew McMaster to the end of his repertory career. The periods of unemployment, the shifting from company to company, the tours in Ireland and later in England might easily have induced a feeling of rootlessness, a lack of security and fear of being threatened with eviction, or might more simply have brought on feelings of subservience to landladies and employed conventional society in general, and vulnerability to intrusion by all manner of people from fellow lodgers to bailiffs and tax-collectors – feelings resulting from comparative poverty and the limited and temporary nature of his stay in the lodgings that served as his living-space.[28] It is indeed to the rep actor's lifestyle, rather than the plays he appeared in, that we must look when considering Pinter's early theme of the threatened inhabitant of the room.[29]

Nevertheless, it might be argued that the thriller and the occasional straight drama provided Pinter – as we have already briefly noted – with a starting-point for his own plays' room sets. For claustrophobic tension the thriller often relies on the vulnerability of a lonely person in an unlocked room. Murderers or potential murderers make their quiet, stealthy entrances into vicarage parlours or the living-rooms of detached houses; detectives and investigators make their necessary presence felt in family homes. In Agatha Christie plays and in others of the thriller genre, as well as in straight drama such as Rattigan's *Separate Tables*, past lovers make secretive entrances through the side doors and French windows of the parlours and dining-rooms of middle-class residences.

Two plays in particular in which Pinter proved successful in leading roles are worth noting for their conventional building-up of suspense towards a potential act of murder; Pinter might be claimed to have learned something from them in the violence often lurking beneath the surface of his plays, occasionally to break out into the open. In the climactic last scene of Agatha Christie's celebrated *Love from a Stranger*, in which Pinter played the role of the maniacal killer, the homicidal inclinations of a known psychopath become increasingly apparent to the intended victim. *The Whole Truth* by Philip Mackie similarly ends with a known murderer just prevented, after a tensely protracted confrontation, from committing a final homicidal act. In both plays the intended victims were alone in a room; in both cases the audience knew of the murderer's intentions well in advance of the would-be victim. In these conventional thrillers part of the tension produced is caused by the sense of confinement that a room's four walls can give. Pinter's early plays to some extent exploit this sense of being trapped – or, more accurately, insecurely cocooned – in a room. Witness Stanley Webber's cry to the intruder McCann in *The Birthday Party*: 'I've explained to you, damn you, that all those years I lived in Basingstoke I never stepped outside the door' (p. 52), and Rose's startled complaint, in *The Room*, to the intruding Riley: 'We're settled down here, cosy, quiet, and our landlord thinks the world of us . . . and you come in and drive him up the wall' (p. 123).

But the plays go much further in introducing the theme of a struggle for territory. Stanley in *The Birthday Party* is seen flattened against the wall of the boarding-house living-room; he is first threatened and then spiritually killed by the two mysterious intruders, who in removing him from his place of shelter render him lifeless. The attic room of *The Caretaker* is the setting for violent, potentially murderous confrontations between the owners and the guest–intruder. The one-room flat occupied by Bert and Rose Hudd, in Pinter's significantly entitled first play, is threatened as it were by outsiders who either want to occupy the room themselves or wish to remove one or both of its occupants. The resultant violent murder of Riley by Hudd can be seen not only in terms of sexual jealousy or racial hatred but also as a response to the apparent threat of usurpation of territory. The rooms in the two thrillers cited are not in themselves seen as jealously guarded territory, nor do they in themselves emanate a sense of menace stemming from a gloomy or neglected appearance. Darkness *is* a temporary feature of the rooms in *The Birthday Party* and *The Room*, while in *The Caretaker* the atmosphere is far from that of the warmth of the hearth, as water drips relentlessly into a dangling bucket! The comparative squalor of these rooms in Pinter's early plays is in direct contrast to the standard conventional middle-class settings of the Agatha Christie and Philip Mackie thrillers, which are typical of the period which saw the last years of the popularity of the French-window drawing-room set. On the other hand, one of the plays in which Pinter acted, Norman King's *The Shadow of Doubt*, does have a relatively squalid setting, and a claustrophobic atmosphere somewhat reminiscent of *The Room* (Bert and Rose appear to know next to nothing of the other rooms of the large house they are in). The setting for Norman King's play is a drab, poorly furnished flat in a Northern city. The scientist who lives there with his wife has taken the flat as a hideout, to escape a threatened charge of treason. A similar kind of claustrophobic effect is found in an American thriller, *Subway in the Sky*, in which a detective hunts down an alleged murderer in the top-storey New York apartment of an isolated divorcee, who to begin with is frightened by the sudden appearance of the hunted man and then is further disturbed that he might be proved a murderer by the second intruder, the detective. In both plays Pinter played the part of an intruder: 'MI5 is at the door in the person of David Baron, black from homburg to toe-cap, a forbidding figure warning the doctor of science of the wrath to come.'[30] But the reference here to an MI5 figure 'at the door' reminds us that, where attention is focused, whether in Pinter or in the rep plays, on a single room, entrances to and exits from that room may be of particular importance.

For Nigel Dennis, it may be remembered, an entrance in a Pinter play is at bottom merely an extension of a drama-school exercise, exploiting the basic dramatic potential of the stage:

> All Pinter plays are like elaborations of the drama school exercise, when the student is told (say), 'You are alone in a room. Suddenly the door opens. You see a man standing there ... OK. Now you improvise the rest.'[31]

What Dennis has seemingly failed to realise is the importance for Pinter's characters of actually crossing the threshold, the differences

made by infiltration of personal territory. Characters' entrances and
exits – via the doors of 'box' interiors – have traditionally been
devised with theatrical effectiveness in mind. The writers of thrillers
and straight dramas in particular have made use of the 'dramatic'
entrance up-centre or the abrupt exit stage left. The French
windows on the back wall would so often open to reveal either the
traditional tennis-player seeking a match or the shadowy figure
from the past, usually making blackmailing demands on the hero or
heroine (*No Escape* by Rhys Davies, Christie's *The Hollow* and
Separate Tables by Rattigan illustrate this point); at the door side-of-
stage would often suddenly stand the inspector or 'MI5 . . . in the
person of David Baron, black from homburg to toe-cap'. Characters
would traditionally, at times almost predictably, make entrances
'on cue', as typified by the extract from Rosemary Casey's *Late Love*
quoted earlier (p. 50). For Pinter the dramatist the importance of
effective entrances and exits is readily apparent:

> What is so different about the stage is that you're just *there*, stuck –
> there are your characters stuck on the stage, you've got to live
> with them and deal with them. I'm not a very inventive writer in
> the sense of using the technical devices other playwrights do –
> look at Brecht! I can't use the stage the way he does, I just haven't
> got that kind of imagination, so I find myself stuck with these
> characters who are either sitting or standing, and they've either
> got to walk out of a door, or come in through a door, and that's
> about all they can do.[32]

Pinter's early plays again are especially relevant here. *A Slight Ache* is
constructed around the entrance of a matchseller into the country-
house home of a well-to-do intellectual and his wife. In this play the
mere act of entering may be said to be equivalent to dispossession –
we are in an ominous surreal world akin to that inhabited by Kullus
and his examiner, in which silence can be a powerful weapon of
usurpation. The theme of intrusion into a person's private world, his
room, and the importance of the entrance of the intruder are
inherently clear in such plays as *The Room*, *The Birthday Party* and
The Caretaker, as well as in the later *No Man's Land*. A sudden knock
at the door following a period of carefully prepared tension or
suspense is a familiar trick used by thriller-writers; Pinter occasionally capitalises on this stage convention by introducing an initial
anti-climactic entrance as a prelude to a second more important

one. In *The Birthday Party* Stanley, afraid of being secretly abducted, has been trying to project his fear onto his landlady Meg, inducing hysteria in the process, when '*a sudden knock on the front door*' brings a dramatic halt to the dialogue. Tension is released upon the immediate discovery that the person calling is no investigator with a wheelbarrow looking for Meg, but the friendly neighbour Lulu with a present. Immediately following Lulu's brief visit, however, the real investigators-*cum*-persecutors arrive more quietly. Yet much is made of their entrance, and Stanley's immediate exit:

> [LULU] *exits . . . .* STANLEY *stands . . . goes into kitchen . . . pause. Enter, by the back door,* GOLDBERG *and* MCCANN. MCCANN *carries two suitcases,* GOLDBERG *a briefcase. They halt inside the door, then walk downstage.* STANLEY, *wiping his face, glimpses their backs through the hatch.* GOLDBERG *and* MCCANN *look round the room.* STANLEY *slips on his glasses, sidles through the kitchen door and out of the back door.* (pp. 36–7)

In the way Pinter has devised the entrance of Goldberg and McCann, sinister and yet not without a touch of humour – McCann struggling with two suitcases, Goldberg relaxed with one briefcase – he has suggested, both through Stanley's spying and quick exit and through their quiet appraisal of the room itself, that their entrance is a kind of infiltration and of great moment. In a lighter vein Pinter plays the same trick of an important entrance following a 'false alarm' entrance in *The Lover*. Immediately before the husband Richard's entrance as Sarah's lover 'Max' the doorbell has rung to admit the lover beloved of many a music-hall comedian from Max Miller downwards, the milkman, with his insistent but refused offer of three jars of clotted cream. The entrance of Richard–Max follows shortly after, with the absurd and macabre effect produced by the audience's realisation that the lover is the same person as the husband under a different name and in different clothing. The introduction of the milkman lightens the tone at this stage of the drama to offset the surreal and menacing effects of Richard–Max's entrance, his obviously suggestive playing of the bongo drums and his assuming the additional role of the smooth-tongued molester who waylays solitary women in parks ('I'm merely asking if you can give me a light' – pp. 174–6).

Pinter can be most innovatory in his handling of entrances and exits. Two examples of each should suffice. There are two kinds of unusual entrances in *The Dumb Waiter* and two exits with a novel touch to them in *No Man's Land*. The introduction of the mechanical device known as a dumb waiter is strictly speaking not a character entrance, but the dumb waiter manages to communicate in a mysteriously personal way, seemingly without human aid or interference, with the two characters of the play. The dumb waiter itself can be seen as a mechanical extension of the mysterious owner of the voice that speaks down the tube to Ben. Its first appearance is most theatrically effective in its mixture of the usual Pinter elements of menace and humour; after Gus and Ben have been discussing in somewhat obscene detail the distasteful aspects of their job of organised assassination

> *There is a loud clatter and racket in the bulge of wall between the beds, of something descending. They grab their revolvers, jump up and face the wall. The noise comes to a stop. . . . Disclosed is a serving-hatch, a 'dumb waiter'.* GUS *peers into the box. He brings out a piece of paper.*

BEN. What is it?
GUS. You have a look at it.
BEN. Read it.
GUS. (*Reading*). Two braised steak and chips. Two sago puddings.
    Two teas without sugar.   (p. 147)

There is a suggestion here, perhaps, of a *deus ex machina* from the world of farce and the music hall. A Delphic oracle removed to working-class Birmingham? The entrance of Gus at the end of the play carries with it its own moment of shock. The audience is expecting the arrival of the long-awaited victim only to find that victim and assassin are the same characters as before; this time the entrance can be seen as being in the firm traditions of the thriller or the gangster film:

> *The door right opens sharply.* BEN *turns his revolver levelled at the door.*
> GUS *stumbles in.*
> *He is stripped of his jacket, waistcoat, tie, holster and revolver.*
> *He stops, body stooping, his arms at his sides.*
> *He raises his head and looks at* BEN.
> *A long silence.*
> *They stare at each other.*

CURTAIN   (p. 165)

The pauses, the long silence help the audience to assimilate the significance of the surprise ending to the play. Perhaps unconsciously Pinter has here been influenced by the cinema – *The Big Sleep* (Howard Hawks, 1946), for example, ends with a body being literally shot through an opening door. Pinter, however, denies the audience the opportunity of seeing the kill.

No Man's Land contains two exits which are truly theatrical in their effect. Both may be seen to have their roots in the farce tradition, though the effects they produce are not purely farcical. One has already been referred to: the end of Act I sees Foster taunting Spooner by switching off the light as he makes his exit, leaving Spooner truly in the dark in a strange house. The other is Hirst's sudden collapse and his undignified crawling off stage earlier in that scene. The exit and the exchanges which lead up to it have their farcical aspects. Viewed from one angle, the decline into drunken stupor and the resulting physical collapse are farcical – with distant echoes of red-nosed comics and variety and music-hall drunk acts such as Al Read's. The vein of comic mockery sustained by Spooner, with his farcical itemising of his wife's physical assets ('My wife . . . had everything. Eyes, a mouth, hair, teeth, buttocks, breasts, absolutely everything. And legs' – p. 31), his bursting into song, and the way he calls attention to Hirst's 'script' ('A metaphor . . . things are looking up' – p. 32), has its affinity with the music-hall comic monologue. Yet the overall effect of the scene with its culminating exit is closer to tragedy. Spooner's offer to 'be your boatman. For if and when we talk of a river we talk of a deep and dank architecture' – p. 33) carries the chilling suggestion of Charon ferrying the souls of the dead across the waters of Lethe. Hirst can only falteringly reply with what has become an obsessive image for him of his own deadly, fruitless existence: 'No man's land ... does not move ... or change ... or grow old ... remains ... forever ... icy ... silent.' Following this short speech Hirst makes a tottering, crawling exit from the room, silently watched by Spooner:

> HIRST loosens his grip on the cabinet, staggers across the room, holds on to a chair.
> *He waits, moves, falls.*
> *He waits, gets to his feet, moves, falls.*
> SPOONER *watches.*
> HIRST *crawls towards the door, manages to open it, crawls out of the door.*
> SPOONER *remains still.* (p. 34)

The kind of effect Pinter is achieving here, within a very different context, is not too far removed from the moments of physical humiliation with which Pinter was familiar from his playing of the roles of Iago and Edgar in Shakespeare's *Othello* and *King Lear*: in *Othello* the mentally tormented tragic hero falls into an epileptic fit watched dispassionately by his antagonist, Iago; in *King Lear* the blind Gloucester stumbles in an act of attempted suicide over a supposed cliff edge observed with pity by his disguised son. In both scenes there is, as Jan Kott has observed in relation particularly to *Lear*, an element of the grotesque, even the farcical, built into the tragic context; an element which ultimately strengthens it. [33]

5 Revaluation: Props, Costumes and Sets

Thus far, Pinter's comments on structure, 'shutting an audience up', working within the confines of the proscenium arch, have provided the basis for discussion, which has indicated some of the distinctive as well as some of the traditional features of his work. But Pinter's acting-experience, as indicated in the opening chapters, took in what Brook describes as 'Rough' and 'Holy' Theatre as well as 'Deadly' Theatre. Part of the purpose of this study is to suggest how in moving away from realism Pinter drew on some of the non-realistic elements to be found in these kinds of theatre. What goes on in the world of Pinter's plays may indeed be, as the playwright himself has suggested, 'realistic', yet, at the same time, 'what I'm doing is not realism'.[1] To elucidate this statement and to indicate something of Pinter's debt to the 'non-realistic' elements of the Rough and Holy Theatre in which he gained his first experience as an actor, it will be appropriate to examine those elements in a play of which the actor must be continuously aware – stage props and costumes, settings, use of stage space and the words he speaks. It will be useful first to attempt to characterise some of the essential differences, some of the broader distinctions to be made, between Rough, Holy and Deadly Theatre in terms of these elements.

The sets, props and costumes generally used in the repertory theatre of Pinter's experience were easily recognisable as belonging to the modern realistic tradition. Well-made plays of the provincial rep world of the fifties usually stressed conventional everyday interior settings and props from familiar social backgrounds. In many cases, as can be readily seen from the much-used Acting Editions of Samuel French, there would be a rigorous attention to the detail of objects to be used, the positioning of furniture, hand props, general decoration and costumes to be worn. The effect achieved by such attention was sometimes reminiscent of that made by the kind of naturalistic play Bernard Shaw satirised as 'a tailor's advertisement making sentimental remarks to a milliner's advertisement in the middle of an upholsterer's and decorator's advertisement'.[2] For the poetic dramas of Shakespeare and Sophocles as staged by Wolfit and McMaster a different kind of effect was demanded from sets, props and costumes. Economic as well as artistic factors led to sets constructed on simpler, more abstract lines; props tended to be kept to a minimum, though an actor such as Wolfit would achieve very powerful effects with a single prop. Elements of Brook's Rough Theatre were, it has been suggested, present in the rather primitive conditions of Anew McMaster's touring company. The trestle tables and backdrops used by McMaster were in essence not far removed from the world of the music hall and the *ad hoc* variety show. Both types of popular theatre needed simple and immediately recognisable visual effects; the focus was on the essential: the man wearing a crown standing in front of a painted column was as instantly comprehensible as a man in a cloth cap in front of a cardboard lamp-post. Props and costumes, of course, were traditionally important to the music-hall comedian: Bud Flanagan's battered hat and extravagant fur coat, Ted Ray's violin, Jimmy James's drooping cigarette were essential components of their acts; they helped in fact to define and heighten the characters these comedians were portraying – Flanagan's cheerful, optimistic zaniness, Ray's intellectual and artistic pretensions, and Jimmy James's sense of identity with the ordinary working man.

In the 'production-line' conditions of the Deadly Theatre little more than the obvious in 'blocking' by the director and in interpretation by the actor can be attempted. As Norman Marshall says in *The Other Theatre*, '[The repertory actor] has time to do no more than learn his positions and his lines . . . . and rely on a collection of superficial tricks and mannerisms to get him through the part.'[3] As for the repertory director, during the first days of rehearsal

> he maps out the production rapidly and efficiently. Then he stops work . . . most repertory producers are not producers at all, they are stage managers. . . . The average time spent on the rehearsal of a play by a weekly repertory company, excluding the dress rehearsal, is fifteen hours.[4]

In such circumstances the point of the remark attributed to Noël Coward, responding to an actor's question about motivation in a

scene from *Nude with Violin*, can be readily appreciated: 'My dear
boy, forget about the motivation. Just say the lines and don't trip
over the furniture.' [5] Pinter's experiences of the classical repertory in
Ireland with McMaster and with Wolfit at the King's Theatre,
Hammersmith, were experiences with old-style actor–managers in
what was tantamount to rep-play conditions. Clearly, so far as the
main body of the supporting cast were concerned, the play was
produced *not* to create maximum effect for their particular scenes, or
to achieve an integrated, subtly and thoughtfully worked-out
organic whole, in which each actor had a crucial part to play, but
rather to achieve an appropriate setting for the leading actor, one
which allowed him to shine. Direction was confined to such basics as
avoiding upstaging or undercutting the leading actor: reference has
been made to Mac's scornful account of the 'bugger' who 'wants to
play Hamlet' and to such simplistic notes as Wolfit's 'you must be
more evil' or 'more noble' and his continued demand for 'Pace,
pace, pace!' [6] But what is clear from accounts by Pinter and others of
Wolfit and McMaster is that they themselves could achieve
powerful and memorable effects in their command of stage
movement, gesture and vocal effect, and could mesmerise both their
fellow actors and the audience in ways which would not have been
possible in the conventionally realistic well-made play. Pinter
himself was impressed by, for example, Wolfit's ability to hold the
pause with his back to the audience, upstage, before swinging
suddenly around flourishing his cloak in *Oedipus at Colonus*; and by
McMaster's skill in acting 'along the spine of a role', and by his
confident subduing a drunken audience in a late-night performance
of *Othello*. [7] If we consider the actor's relationship to other actors and
to the audience in Rough Theatre with particular reference to those
forms of it exemplified in the popular traditions of the music-hall
comic monologue and cross-talk act it is to note perhaps three
features of importance for the solo performer in particular. First, the
audience represents the indispensable partner of the comedian;
without audience response the identity of the performer vanishes.
Since the audience validates the performer's identity, care is taken
to cajole, woo, rebuke, appeal to the audience as the act develops.
Secondly, with regard to the cross-talk act, the funny man's
indispensable partner is, of course, the stooge or feed man, though
the comic partner plays off the stooge to the audience. Essential in
such pairings is the concept of contrast, such that the one is the foil to
the other, physically and in terms of mental agility – fat and thin,

tall and short, quick-witted and stupid, braggart and parasite. The element of role-playing is a very important feature of the music-hall comedian's art: the comic plays inside yet outside his role, building an imaginary situation and involving himself in it, switching roles, keeping the audience alert, involved, but able to enjoy the 'gamesmanship' which is a result of the constant referral to audience, the role-changing from 'actor' to commentator. An obvious example relevant here would be Max Miller, whose act mainly consisted of a list of 'sincerely' told outrageous stories about himself or close relations, interspersed with catch phrases purporting to comment on the material, and mock-serious admonitions to the audience for perceiving sexual innuendo in the material and finding it amusing.

The characteristics of the language used in the three distinct kinds of theatre examined here are less easy to pin down. In the repertory theatre of the 1950s, however, a sizeable majority of the thrillers, farces and romances that characterised that theatre were written within the literary conventions of the well-made play: dialogue was rarely naturalistic and colloquial but aimed at being selectively respectable and elegant in subject-matter and construction. Characters in well-made plays tended to speak in conventionally accepted class idioms and consequently often became easily reduced to the 'type' summaries which often featured in the Producer's Notes in Samuel French's Acting Editions. Demands made by the censor and Rattigan's middle-brow and rather straight-laced Aunt Edna figure produced language which was often of a stereotyped middle-class respectability tending to favour the proverbial phrase, the well-worn idiom, the polite linguistic norm. Upper- or working-class characters were generally treated in even more stereotyped fashion: aristocratic eccentrics, for example, were often given elliptical, curt or quaint modes of address; Cockneys were almost always bright and garrulous, Northerners more dour and to the point. With the exception of more sophisticated playwrights such as Coward, Rattigan and Priestley, most writers of the post-war period tended to have little concern for a precise, witty use of language; they preferred on the whole a more utilitarian approach to dialogue, whose main aim was to reveal in grammatically correct terms plain facts about characters and plot.

The rich and varied language of the Shakespearian plays that featured in the repertoire of McMaster and Wolfit could not be further removed from the prose conventionalities, the somewhat banal use of language, in the standard rep play. While it is beyond the scope of this analysis to attempt to characterise that language in all its range and complexity, there are two features of it which, I suggest, relate interestingly to Pinter's own plays, and to which his own playing of the roles of Iago and Edmund in particular would have directed his attention. First, it is a language which can accommodate with perfect naturalness both the colloquial exchanges of everyday life and the moments of poetic intensity and high passion, where a soliloquy or uninterrupted solo passage offers a challenge to the vocal range and strength of the actor. Pinter's own references to the memorable vocal effects achieved by McMaster in *Othello* remind us of how one actor of Pinter's acquaintance met that challenge:

> His voice was unique: in my experience of an unequalled range. A bass of extraordinary echo, resonance and gut, and remarkable sweep up into tenor, when the note would hit the back of the gallery and come straight back, a brilliant stunning sound. [8]

The flexibility of the language is one factor enabling the play to operate on different levels of realism, and to move between them. The other feature is a more particular one relating to the verbal skills and rhetorical persuasiveness with which the dramatist endows certain tricksters and manipulators in the plays: Iago, Richard III (or, outside the Shakespearian repertory, Jonson's Mosca and Face). Language is here used as a weapon in insidious acts of deception, persuasion and flattery; words are aggressive counters used in dangerous or deadly games played with others.

The Rough Theatre of music-hall comedy (and its radio derivative) offers a different kind of linguistic resourcefulness. A wide variety of modes of address, idioms, dialects and registers is typical of the language of the music-hall comedian. Parody, innuendo, the multiplicity of roles adopted by the comedian all point towards a use of language that is varied enough to exist on different referential levels simultaneously. As would be expected in a form of popular entertainment, the language is mainly familiar, of a colloquial idiom, with frequent use of the everyday cliché delivered in an apparently impromptu conversational manner, with all the digressions, repetitions, stoppings and startings of ordinary talk. For example, here is Max Miller in full flow:

We started to walk across the desert – no, turn it up, what's the matter with you – no, well ... No, when a chap's talking – no, it's true ... well ... Git out of it! Well ... We started to walk across the desert – five days and five nights we were walking. We came to a tent – we stood outside the tent – I wouldn't go in – two thousand years old, she was! [9]

Often, however, the music-hall comedian would take a delight in the possibilities of language in creating a rich and strange reality. Through using language in a surreal or metaphorical manner, comedians of the music hall, and its derivative the radio comedy or variety show, were able to present to an audience two levels of meaning simultaneously – the innocent and the suggestively sexual.

She said, 'Son, you're going out into the world and I'm going to tell you everything.' I said, 'Go on, Mother, tell me. I have no shame, tell me.' She said, 'It's not Father Christmas who puts the toys in your stocking.'

Of course I knew all the time – I'll tell you why, because one morning when I woke up I found a bicycle in my stocking and I was riding down the road and I knocked a poor old lady over, and when she picked herself up she said to me, 'Can't you ring the bell?' I said, 'Yes, I can ring the bell, but I can't ride the bike.' [10]

Much of the bawdy humour of Max Miller is truly an example of 'a language . . . where under what is said, another thing is being said'. [11] Thus the language of suggestion is an important facet of the illegitimate theatre comedian, as is the use of language as hyperbole to build up outrageous images and suggestions, and the use of language as camouflage, a thinly disguised stratagem to conceal the real feelings and thoughts of the character – as demonstrated by Tony Hancock, a leading exponent of preposterous bluffing of outrageous hypocrisy. Of equal importance to the stand-up comic or the double act is the use of comic effects obtained from the accumulation of epithets, repetition of phrasing, and carefully constructed stories of gags leading to a well-timed punch line or bathetic end line. These artists of the illegitimate theatre depended for their livelihood upon more than mere playing with words; the best of them were able to use language in precise and carefully calculated forms as an essential part of their acts.

A discussion on the use Pinter makes of props and costumes might usefully start with the previously quoted recollection by Pinter of Wolfit's cloak effect in *Oedipus at Colonus*. Wolfit managed to impress upon Pinter the power that an actor can achieve by skilled use of an object or costume property; Pinter acknowledges his debt to Wolfit as a playwright:

> He held the moment until one's stomach was truly trembling and the cloak came round; a tremendous swish that no one else has been able to achieve I think. And the savagery and power that emerged from such a moment was extraordinary . . . you haven't got the cloak but you do have the glass.[12]

In the contemporary worlds of Pinter's dramas, ordinary household objects, often those to be found in a realistic well-made play of the post-war period – spectacles, newspapers, cups and saucers, drinking-glasses, cigars and cigarettes, domestic appliances from telephones to vacuum cleaners – can often be said to assume a dramatic importance as weighty as that achieved by such an actor as Wolfit with classical props and costumes. The audience's attention is often made to focus on a stage property or costume, which thereby acquires a special significance, often symbolic or poetic. One of the characters in *The Homecoming*, Lenny, comments interestingly on the power of ordinary objects to cause a stir, to disturb, to change things. He wonders, at the beginning of presumably his first conversation with his sister-in-law, Ruth, whether it was the clock he is holding that woke him up in bed:

> I've been having a bit of a rough time with this clock. The tick's been keeping me up. The trouble is I'm not all that convinced it was the clock. I mean there are lots of things which tick in the night, don't you find that? All sorts of objects, which, in the day, you wouldn't call anything else but commonplace. They give you no trouble. But in the night any given one of a number of them is liable to start letting out a bit of a tick.   (p. 44)

Pinter is indeed himself adept at giving a dramatic significance to 'all sorts of objects', which normally 'you wouldn't call anything else but commonplace'. This late-night meeting between Lenny and Ruth may serve as an example of Pinter's ability to create significant dramatic moments through focusing the audience's attention on props and costumes. The clock that is placed in front of Lenny serves to indicate, on a very simple level, the lateness of the hour, just as much as Lenny's later comment on the difference in dress between the two of them ('Isn't it funny? I've got my pyjamas on and you're fully dressed.'–p. 45). More importantly the clock serves as a pretext for Lenny to indulge in verbal games, a humorous but faintly sinister mock-philosophical line of talk: 'So ... all things being equal ... this question of me saying it was the clock that woke me up, well, that could very easily prove something of a false hypothesis' (p. 44).

What Lenny is by implication drawing attention to here is the probable fact that it is the visitors' late arrival that has disturbed him, and more importantly, perhaps, the mysterious temporary leaving of the house by Ruth, which he has seen disturb her husband. Lenny is intrigued by the person he finds himself talking to in the early hours of the morning, and the clock is there for her to see a reason for his staying up to talk to her. The glass of water he then proffers her is instantly made to seem as carrying more than usual dramatic significance. Lenny has previously adopted a half-humorous, half-challenging mode of address when offering Ruth an 'aperitif', only to reveal that there is no alcohol in the house. Nevertheless, the glass of water which Ruth accepts is treated as if it contained a more substantial, sophisticated drink. It is this element of play-acting – part-amusing, part-menacing – that causes a direct confrontation between the two of them:

LENNY. . . . . And now perhaps I'll relieve you of your glass.
RUTH. I haven't quite finished.
LENNY. You've consumed quite enough, in my opinion.
RUTH. No I haven't.
LENNY. Quite sufficient, in my opinion.
RUTH. Not in mine, Leonard.   (p. 49)

Then, having thus frugally entertained his brother's wife, and having tried to intimidate or at least impress her with macabre and aggressively suggestive talk, Lenny is forced onto the defensive by being in a sense hoist with his own petard. Equally outrageously Ruth offers to pour the water down Lenny's throat, having threatened, 'If you take the glass ... I'll take you.' The glass is thus seen as a weapon in a game of sexual bluff and intimidation, a seemingly harmless but ultimately powerful counter in a deeply felt struggle for dominance.

For the most part even props of interest to the writer of more sensational drama, such as daggers and guns, are less melodramatically and unambiguously used in Pinter's plays. The production of a knife or a gun by a murderer in a whodunnit or thriller is nearly always at a dramatically climactic moment with the obvious result of murder or thwarted murder; in Pinter the production of a gun or a knife is often to be seen in the form of mere gesture – certainly no one ever actually gets killed by a weapon in a Pinter play, if we discount the reported stabbing of Roote and Miss Cutts in *The Hothouse*. Pinter most closely approaches the kind of tension evoked in a thriller when Davies, the tramp, produces a weapon in the third act of *The Caretaker* (p. 76). The wielder of the knife, however, is rendered impotent by an implacable silence on Aston's part and the threat of violence is removed. Previously in the same play Davies's first resort to his weapon, when facing the other brother, Mick, is a typical example of the fine balance of moods – violent tension and humour – for which Pinter's plays have been noted. Mick's casual, mocking attitude to the potentially dangerous situation is tantamount to an insistence that his would-be assailant is merely play-acting: 'Eh, you're not thinking of doing any violence on me, are you? You're not the violent sort, are you?' (p. 55). If there is any dramatic precedent for Mick's behaviour here it is in the world of gangster films, in which the surprised hero – often Humphrey Bogart! – remains 'cool' and talks his way, patronisingly and wittily, out of trouble. What follows in Pinter's play is a kind of farcical *reductio ad absurdum* when Mick shares a snack with Davies, after commending the tramp for 'impressing' him. The world of the popular gangster movie is perhaps more readily suggested by the situation presented in *The Dumb Waiter*, in which the two assassins' guns are very much in evidence throughout the play. But the play achieves its own special kind of effect from a mixing of elements of the circus (the characters as knockabout clowns), the thriller and the music-hall cross-talk patter act. Hence the necessity for an ambivalent ending when the assassins face each other as potential victim and killer. Knives are also used as potential weapons in *The Hothouse* and *The Collection*. In both cases Pinter makes the brandishing of knives into a mock, ritualised gesture, in a much more stylised way than elsewhere. The bickering Roote, Lush and Gibbs, who casually discuss the possibility of murder as well as indulging in verbal role-playing games, suddenly form an absurd three-way fighting-stance pattern with knives drawn at the ready.

The surreal nature of the situation is further emphasised when their belligerent attitudes are shattered by unidentified amplified humanlike sound-effects to which the three characters react simultaneously in identical puzzled fashion, immediately forgetting their confrontation (p. 135). The worlds of farce and thriller are merged less effectively here, however, since the characters are, as Pinter himself has acknowledged, two-dimensional figures in a purposefully satirical play.[13] In the knife-drawing sequence the worlds of farce, melodrama and the puppet theatre seem to be merged! Pinter often achieves his best effects with props (as with dialogue) when there is an ambivalence of menace and humour, a successful fusion of elements from a combination of Deadly, Holy and Rough Theatre. The 'mock duel' which James tries to set up in *The Collection* with a cheese knife and fruit knife as weapons is more effective since it involves a largely unspoken trial of virility between the two men concerned, one of whom has allegedly been cuckolded by the other. The ambiguities and doubts which surround Bill's possible seduction of James's wife preclude a more serious confrontation than the one indulged in, which ends with the token wounding of Bill by a satisfied James, gratified to be for once assured of a change in situation by the visual evidence of Bill's cut hand: 'Ah yes. Now you've got a scar on your hand. You didn't have one before, did you?' (pp. 151–3).

Ambivalent effects are also caused by Pinter's use of drums in two of his plays. In *The Lover* the tapping of a bongo drum by Richard to establish a mood of seduction in his consciously adopted role as his wife's lover is the prelude to a cat-and-mouse piece of ritualised courtship business by the couple, culminating in '*Wild beats of their fingers tangling*' (pp. 175–6). There is unquestionably here an echo of vaudeville business or material from a pantomime sketch in which crude and obvious sound or orchestral effects are used to accompany a palpably contrived seduction scene. Nevertheless, the drumming manages also to produce the more serious, macabre effect of a husband and wife playing their by-now necessary game of double identity in order to preserve their relationship. Pinter thus manages to blend a farcical element of the illegitimate theatre into his realistic drama. A similar richness of effect is found in Pinter's use of the drum that Meg presents to Stanley in *The Birthday Party*. Two scenes from this play are relevant here: the end of Act I, in which Stanley beats the toy drum in Meg's presence first playfully then more menacingly (p. 46); and during the party scene, when Stanley beats the side of his now-broken drum in a state of deranged hysteria (pp. 73–5). Pinter's skill can be highlighted by comparing these scenes with one which seems to have influenced him (as Leslie Smith in 'Pinter the Player' points out[14]) in Priestley's *Mr Kettle and Mrs Moon*. In this scene the frustrated bank-manager Kettle bangs away on a coalscuttle with a child's drumstick in an attempt to conjure up a feeling of lost innocence and a soon-to-be-found sense of emancipation from his restricting professional role in society. Priestley renders his character's drumming less effective than Pinter's by introducing accompanying music from a record-player, and there is a more contrived air to the Priestley scene, which succeeds only in appearing rather ludicrous in its obvious striving for effect. This contrasts with the menace and pathos engendered by Pinter on the two occasions when he has Stanley, the would-be concert pianist, frenziedly beating his landlady's birthday gift in increasing frustration and with growing anger at his own pathetic situation. The scene at the end of Act i, in particular, may be studied in relation to realistic drama as well as to popular theatre and the ritual, poetic drama. The realistic level arises naturally out of the already-established relationship between the maternal, soft-hearted but intellectually barren Meg and her surrogate son, Stanley, who makes ineffectual attempts to maintain his dignity in the knowledge of having failed as a musician and, seemingly, as a social being. The offering and acceptance of the amusing but humiliating gift is presented with the desultory stop-and-start rhythms of everyday conversation. In addition, the Rough Theatre's music-hall double act, or possibly even the world of the pierrot and clown, is hinted at as Meg Boles first insists on presenting her lodger with a parcel on the day she resolutely maintains, despite contradiction, is his birthday:

MEG. . . . You mustn't be sad today. It's your birthday.

A pause.

STANLEY. (*dumbly*). Uh?

MEG. It's your birthday, Stan. I was going to keep it a secret until tonight.

STANLEY. No.

MEG. It is. I've brought you a present. (*She goes to the sideboard, picks up the parcel, and places it on the table in front of him.*) Here. Go on. Open it.

STANLEY. What's this?
MEG. It's your present.
STANLEY. This isn't my birthday, Meg.
MEG. Of course it is. Open your present.

> *He stares at the parcel, slowly stands, and opens it. He takes out a boy's drum.*

STANLEY (*flatly*). It's a drum. A boy's drum.
MEG (*tenderly*). It's because you haven't got a piano. (pp. 45–6).

The combination of pathos and the almost surreal humour that arises from a character's obstinate refusal to be enlightened is a well-known one in the popular theatrical tradition. There are faint echoes here of a typical routine of variety or circus clowns: the mischievous clown promises a 'nice surprise' box for the sad clown; after a short, tantalising 'build-up' the surprise is revealed as a squirt in the eye or a punch on the nose from a jack-in-the-box. I am also reminded of the Dick Bentley and June Whitfield 'Ron and Eth' sketches from the popular radio comedy series of the fifties, *Take it from Here*. Meg's insistent, smothering maternal attentions and Stanley's diminution to boyhood status are reminiscent of the richly comic relationship that existed between the ever-hopeful mollycoddling Eth and her eternally hopeless and immature fiancé Ron, whose interest in life could be aroused only by presents that might attract a young schoolboy. The half-comic, half-pathetic mood of the Pinter play, however, changes radically though imperceptibly at first as Stanley seems unsure of how to react, of what role to adopt to meet the situation. It seems he is to play the clown's role, as, resigned to his absurdly humiliating gift, he places the drum round his neck and begins to beat it gently, marching dutifully for Meg's benefit round the table. On the second circuit round the table the drum becomes a more primitive, ritualistic symbol of hatred and defiance; we are indeed now closer to the ritual, classical theatre of heightened emotion than to the circus ring:

> *he begins to go round the table a second time. Halfway round the beat becomes erratic, uncontrolled. Meg expresses dismay. He arrives at her chair, banging the drum, his face and the drumbeat now savage and possessed.* (p. 46)

Stanley's drum has become a veritable millstone round his neck; his frenzied beating of it merely emphasises his impotence and perhaps suggests that he is 'summoning up his attackers out of the darkness'.[15] In such a way Pinter achieves one of his most effective theatrical moments, in its own anti-heroic way equivalent to the 'savagery and power' he had seen produced by Wolfit's manipulation of the cloak in *Oedipus at Colonus*.

The world of the cocktail comedy or sophisticated light drama of the fifties rep is recalled in a number of scenes by Pinter dealing with the dispensing and consuming of drinks. In the comedies of Coward and in fifties thrillers and drawing-room comedies, the social ritual of pouring and imbibing alcoholic drinks usually served as a visual reminder of the manners and polite decorum of middle- or upper middle-class society – in other words, it was a mere embellishment to the drama. Pinter's treatment of drinking 'business', it could be argued, is at times less in line with the world of the well-made play than with the theatre of the music hall or that of the classical poetic drama. In *No Man's Land* the constant pouring of the whisky, vodka and champagne which so annoyed Clive James in his review of the television version of the original production (he claimed the cocktail-party element was mere theatrical self-indulgence[16]) is immediately relevant to the question of Hirst's almost tragic alcoholic refuge from a guilty past and a barren present, and later pertinent to the same character's paradoxically mendicant role in his relationships with his servants and his guest (when Briggs adamantly refuses to serve his master with a drink, he gives Spooner the opportunity of playing the servant role – pp. 80–1). Pinter at a later point focuses on the ritualistic nature of polite social drinking and mocks it in impolite terms. Foster has just refused Briggs's offer of a glass of champagne and provokes a rebuke from his master, Hirst:

> HIRST. Oh come on, be sociable. Be sociable. Consort with the society to which you're attached. To which you're attached as if by bonds of steel. Mingle.
>
> BRIGGS pours a glass for FOSTER.
>
> FOSTER. It isn't even lunchtime.
> BRIGGS. The best time to drink champagne is before lunch, you cunt. (p. 85)

In the early play *The Hothouse*, by way of contrast, the knockabout farce of the illegitimate theatre is in evidence when twice Roote mechanically throws his whisky in his subordinate Lush's face – custard-pie fashion – whilst Lush steadily refuses to acknowledge the insults and refills his superior's glass (p. 89). In this play, which was orginally shelved by Pinter for being 'heavily satirical and . . . quite useless. . . . The characters were so purely card-board',[17] the props, like the words and actions of the characters, are used much more arbitrarily and their effectiveness is consequently lessened; the electrodes placed on Lamb's head for electric-shock therapy are used in a context as farcical and absurd as the more obvious, simple practical joke of the exploding cigar that Roote receives from a vengeful Lush (pp. 64, 139).

The slapstick comic element is utilised in the more seriously drawn, realistic world of *The Caretaker* (written immediately after *The Hothouse*) with correspondingly increased effectiveness. For example, the three characters' bag-passing routine in the second act has been generally observed as having theatrical antecedents in Beckett and the music hall.[18] Pinter's use here of this piece of somewhat ritualised stage business can be seen as theatrically and artistically more effective than *The Hothouse*'s corresponding three-handed confrontation (see p. 77), in which Roote, Gibbs and Lush form a ludicrously melodramatic, potentially lethal triangle. Mick's continued snatching of Davies's bag and Aston's persistent retrieving of it may of course be presented simply like a hat-switching routine from the music hall, but the business is potentially much more effective when the balance between naturalism and ritual is kept; in this way the humour to be gained from the action does not prevent the audience from perceiving a precisely observed character portrayal in dumb show: highlighted are Mick's insistent and playful terrorism, Aston's slow but patient charity and Davies's vulnerable ineptitude.

Where Pinter often goes beyond the conventions of the modern well-made play in his use of props can also be seen in certain relatively minor, insignificant moments. For example, McCann in *The Birthday Party* seems merely, at first glance, to be idling away his time in his absurdly meticulous tearing of a newspaper into strips. We might at first be inclined to agree with Goldberg that 'It's childish, it's pointless' (p. 85). But there is obviously some point in the activity so far as McCann is concerned: he reproves Stanley three times for harmlessly touching his strips of paper. The playwright – like McCann – is not simply indulging himself by presenting stage business for the sake of meaningless by-play. When at the end of the play the newspaper-clippings drop to the floor at Petey's feet, after the departure of the automaton-like Stanley, newly decked out in pinstripes, Petey can only look wonderingly down at them. McCann's careful destructiveness is complete: he has helped to make a neat 'job' of Stanley, and in a subtly symbolic way the shredded pieces of paper highlight McCann's clinical thoroughness as a wielder of destruction as well as his near-pathological edginess throughout the play. Comparably symbolic use of props on this minor level is quite a rare feature of the rep plays Pinter acted in. A comparison may, however, be made between McCann and his newspaper and, say, Agatha Christie's detective Hercule Poirot and his playing-card house. In *Peril at End House*, in which Pinter played important roles in Bournemouth and Torquay, one act opens with Poirot calmly trying to piece together certain clues concerning a fatal shooting-incident whilst patiently building up a house of cards. This piece of stage business is effective in a simple way: the symbolism relating to the character is more readily discernible than is the case with Harold Pinter's McCann. In the main, however, props in detective plays are often synonymous with the crossword-puzzle clues to which Pinter alludes in his previously cited remark about the nature of the traditional 'explained-away' drama. The cufflinks of a leading character in *The Whole Truth*, for instance, help to establish a murderer, just as the more substantial wheelchair of a female character involved in the murders in *Peril at End House* initially helps to divert suspicion away from her. These are props which, like the vanity case from the play of the same title, are important 'clues' in the thriller genre's game of detection and surprise, and they have the same importance, on a literal, prosaic level, as 'exhibit A' in a police court.

Pinter gradually learned to use stage properties as sparingly as possible in order to realise more fully the poetic, symbolic side of his dramas. The rooms of *The Caretaker* and *The Birthday Party* are more detailed than the more economically 'furnished' sets of *The Homecoming*, *Old Times* and *No Man's Land*. *Landscape* and *Silence* are, of course, conceived in a more purely abstract, poetic way, all but dispensing with props and set. Yet, as we have seen, the two early plays mentioned can afford many examples of the symbolic use of stage objects. The cluttered attic of *The Caretaker* may be seen as a spatial extension of Aston's character. Aston's inability to organise his environment tells us as much about his character as do his incessant, fruitless attempts to mend a particular plug, which represents one minute item from all the lumber which surrounds him. The settings and properties of the naturalistically conceived plays of the fifties rep tended to be purely ornamental, as has been suggested earlier in this section; they merely served to evoke, albeit vividly, the environment of the appropriate social class. In French's edition of *Rebecca*, for example, there is a four-page list of items of furniture and general properties,[19] ranging from chintz armchairs to *Tatler* magazines, from a grand piano to a painted enamel bowl of roses; a dustpan and brush, and duster, are assigned to the Second Maid, whilst the First Maid is obliged to use a duster solely; menus, pencils, cigarette cases, candlesticks, two walking-sticks and a 'virginity disc' represent just a small selection of personal properties to be made available to a typical repertory company attempting to reproduce West End attention to naturalistic detail. Very few of these many objects are given any symbolic significance in the play, and when they are, as in the case of the china cupid ornament that Mrs de Winter breaks in the second scene of the play, the symbolism is most carefully and emphatically explicated:

> MAXIM. Oh, damn that infernal cupid! Do you really think I care whether it's in ten thousand pieces or not?
> MRS DE WINTER. Was it very valuable?
> MAXIM. Heaven knows ...
> MRS DE WINTER. Are all the things on the mantelpiece valuable?
> MAXIM. Yes, I believe so.
> MRS DE WINTER. Perhaps – they were put on the mantelpiece here when you were first married.
> MAXIM. Perhaps they were.
> MRS DE WINTER. I suppose the cupid was put there then?
> MAXIM. Yes. As a matter of fact, I believe it was a wedding present. Rebecca knew a lot about china.
> MRS DE WINTER. I see. That's why it's so precious.[20]

The heavy underlining of the symbolism attending the breakage is, it must be admitted, balanced by the tension built up by Mrs de Winter's understandable insistence on ascertaining her husband's true feelings on the matter. The audience is left in no doubt of the link between Max's continued obsessive feelings towards his first wife and the continued apparent treasuring of so many objects associated with her. In Pinter's *The Caretaker*, by way of contrast, Aston's reproduction Buddha is deliberately smashed by his brother Mick in a state of desperate frustration (p. 83). Initially this act of violence may be seen as a piece of glib symbolism, a rather melodramatic *coup de théâtre* providing a last-act climax: Mick, the evil brother, destroys the relationship with the good brother Aston in destroying what is tantamount to a symbol of Aston's peacefulness and serenity. Pinter, however, leaves the significance of this violent act typically open to question. The playwright has, it may be remembered, often denied the existence of consciously applied symbolism in his plays: 'I wouldn't know a symbol if I saw one. I don't see that there's anything very strange about *The Caretaker*, for instance. . . . It seems to me a very straightforward and simple play'[21]; and the complexities and ambiguities inherent in his characters, their words and their actions, preclude any easy solutions as to their meaning. In the case of the smashed Buddha, causes and effects are complex: its destroyer commits the act of violence apparently as an aggressive gesture towards Davies, whom he has just tried to dismiss from his life; yet after the act Mick's anxieties are directed towards himself and his brother. On Aston's entrance, however, the brothers, rather than recognise an irrevocable impasse in their relationship, paradoxically smile at one another and Mick inarticulately attempts to apologise. What does become clear, however, following the smashing of the Buddha, is the air of finality and repudiation that now marks the brothers' relationships with their lodger, Davies.

After drawing attention to particular objects that at first glance are mere embellishments to naturalistically detailed sets, but later are seen to bear some symbolic significance, we might profitably return to the subject of the nature of the sets Pinter envisaged for his plays. Pinter and his directors and stage-designers have come to realise the difficulties involved in designing a set capable of reflecting the plays' fine balance between a carefully structured 'naturalistic' presentation of contemporary life and the evocation of a more poetic, abstract, fundamental world. Early in Pinter's career as a playwright naturalism seemed more important to him with regard to sets. He has, however, confessed to an initial uncertainty in this matter: 'The only really bad experience I've had was *The Birthday Party*; I was so green and gauche. . . . Anyway, for things like stage design I didn't know how to cope, and I didn't know how to talk to the director.'[22]

Eventually, however, Pinter felt the need to reduce the originally highly detailed set for his first full-length play to a short list of essential items: three doors, a window, a hatch, and table and chairs. *The Caretaker*, however, is not reduced to the level of mere naturalism by its detailed, if not cluttered, set. There is a bleakness and a strangeness which emanates from the brothers' attic room, in which a piece of sack and a suspended bucket attempt to ward off the winter's wind and rain. It is not too difficult or far-fetched to imagine the room as a microcosm of man's ineffectual attempts to establish order over chaos. Some of Pinter's early sets are more obviously reflections of his dual interest in the realistic tradition and the symbolic, more poetic theatre. *A Slight Ache*, for example, most closely resembles the favourite affluent middle-class setting of the West End play used by the rep companies Pinter worked for in the 1950s. Yet Pinter insists on 'a minimum of scenery and props' (p. 169), and, while this may be seen as a necessary result of the work's origin as a radio play, it also helps to underline the dream-like, poetical quality of the play as a whole. *The Homecoming* has a strong symbolic significance attached to it, and this has been noted especially by its first producer, Peter Hall, who insisted on a set uncluttered by naturalistic detail. Critics have pertinently commented on the symbolism behind the first important feature of the large room of Max's old North London house. Leslie Smith recalls the work of the producer and designer of the original Aldwych production:

> Peter Hall describes the set which John Bury designed to realise Pinter's intentions as 'simple, antiseptic, grey, dead . . . it reminded me of an old butcher who used to be covered in blood and is now in a sterile world . . . from which women have been excluded'. The back wall, as Pinter's stage direction indicates, has been knocked down to make an open living area: 'A square arch shape remains.' Bury's first design had a large beam across where the wall had been knocked down. Pinter's response was 'that's right but it's too explicit'. What replaced it was a girder, purely functional and plastered over. The result was to give the scene an uncluttered, monumental quality, to create, in effect, an appropriate setting for ritual drama . . . .[23]

Notwithstanding this concern to produce a setting for a more poetic, 'ritual' drama (Leslie Smith imaginatively makes a comparison with Aeschylus's bloody House of Atreus), there remains the element of realism. Just as the opulent and extensively furnished Manderley of *Rebecca* tells us much about the tastes of de Winter's deceased first wife, the domestic attentions of his housekeeper, who remains obsessively loyal to Rebecca's memory, and, simply, the elegance of the social class to which he belongs, so the vast open room of *The Homecoming* does much to present the stark world of an all-male family capable of demolishing a wall of their main living-room but not of decking it with any finery alien to their nature. In a sense the gap left by the death of the only female in the family is reflected by the stark gap left in the design of their living-area. When Pinter turns to the more elegant and affluent worlds of *Old Times* and *No Man's Land* he again is concerned with the need for sets reduced to essentials – walls, doors and the minimum of furniture. The poetic 'atmospheric' world of *Old Times* is observed in the clean, almost clinical surroundings of modern furnishing, and the barren but prosperous world of Hirst in *No Man's Land* is reflected in the '*well but sparsely furnished*' set. In this set everything has its own quick, symbolic role to play. Pinter specifies '*heavy curtains*' which can easily shut out the reality of the outside world for Hirst and guard him in his 'lighthouse' in the ivory region of Hampstead. The drinks cabinet is placed centre-stage – justifiably so in symbolic terms, since it contains Hirst's main means of escape from present reality to the icy, silent haven of his 'no man's land'. The two other features of the room mentioned in Pinter's introductory note are the '*wall of bookshelves*' (aptly, for symbolic purposes, to one side, representing Hirst's past literary achievements and source of power) and '*a strong and comfortable straight-backed chair*', which may be said to represent Hirst's throne (p. 9).

The appearance of the actor on the stage, his costume and its significance may also be considered with reference to Pinter's own acting-experience. In the Holy Theatre of the classical repertoire the chief characters were of visually distinctive appearance. We have already noted Wolfit's particular concern for suitability of costume and Pinter's especial memory of him as Oedipus using his cloak to create a theatrical moment. Costume is used in Shakespeare's plays for purposes of disguise, as, for example, in the role of Edgar in *King Lear*, which Pinter played on the Irish tour with McMaster; costume and physical appearance may also belie the true nature of the character: the 'honesty' of Iago, another of Pinter's roles with McMaster, is conveyed by the bluff soldierly appearance of the man, so much at odds with his true nature. Costume in the Rough Theatre of the music hall could be of various kinds: there were the smartly suited double acts, such as Jewell and Warriss; the bizarrely dressed comedians, such as Bud Flanagan, Max Miller and Arthur English; and those whose costume and props were carefully assembled to create a 'persona' – most famously, in the Chaplin tramp figure, but also in the creations of such performers as Cardew Robinson with his schoolboy 'cad' image. In the Deadly Theatre of the provincial rep the thriller or detective play offers examples of the visually distinctive inspector – intruder figure, either in uniform or in regulation plain-clothes coat and hat, like David Baron's MI5 man 'black from homburg to toe-cap' in *The Shadow of Doubt*, and examples of appearance and costume belying the character's true nature: the homicidal maniac in *Love from a Stranger* looks a respectable and law-abiding citizen. Some of the romantic comedies in the provincial repertoire (*Affairs of State*, *Late Love* and *Down Came a Blackbird*) offer examples of transformation scenes from 'ugly duckling' to 'romantic lead', through some minor but significant alterations of appearance.

How then do Pinter's plays make use of the actor's costume and appearance, and are there any points of connection here with the plays in which he acted? There is little at first glance in Pinter's plays that could provoke comparison with the visually distinctive garb of the tragic hero, the king or the prince. Visually as well as linguistically Pinter's plays have a realistic context and frame of reference; they are set in a recognisably contemporary world with characters dressed in the everyday clothes of that world. Perhaps as the plays move beyond that frame of reference and tap deeper levels of meaning the visual 'ordinariness' of the characters involved creates its own particular effect: thus the bizarre acts of persecution and murder in *The Hothouse* are made more chilly and possibly more amusing by their involving characters whose dress suggests they are no more or less than conventionally minded bureaucrats. Then, in the Shakespearian repertoire (as indeed in the modern thriller) the matter of a character's appearance hiding his true nature is a fairly clear-cut one: a matter of a mask of respectability covering a person's evil designs, the look of the innocent flower hiding the serpent beneath. The true nature of any of Pinter's characters is ultimately unknowable or indefinable; ambiguity in Pinter's plays tends to work against this kind of straightforward mask/face contrast, since, as has been shown in part, the characters in Pinter's plays explore linguistically a variety of versions of themselves and their experiences. Nevertheless, the effect of menace or surprise that can be gained by use of a character whose appearance is at odds with certain facets of his behaviour or nature is sometimes apparent in Pinter. In *The Birthday Party* the besuited Goldberg and McCann do not belie by their appearance Meg's repeated description of them as 'gentlemen' (pp. 29, 30, 44). Their subsequent acts of psychological terrorism and their bizarre verbal games played with each other and with or against Stanley are in direct contrast to their normal, respectable attire; it is of course in their interest as members of whatever sinister organisation they belong to that they should not draw immediate attention to themselves by their appearance.

Clearly, if we consider costume in Pinter's plays in relation to the Rough Theatre of the music hall we would not expect to find within the realistic context the more bizarre costumes which some comedians have made their trademark. None the less, just as certain elements of the music hall have been seen (by Peter Davison pre-eminently) in the linguistic exchanges of the plays, occasionally the characters' appearance too may be seen to reflect music-hall practice.

Much of the comic effectiveness of the most famous Pinter tramp figure, Davies in *The Caretaker*, derives from his appearance. Pinter is careful to give explicit detail: '*a worn brown overcoat, shapeless trousers, a waistcoat, vest, no shirt, and sandals*' (p. 16). In the play great attention is recurringly paid to his physical appearance, often as a source of laughter, and occasionally with resulting tension and a sense of menace. Davies in long-johns, without his trousers, getting ready for bed and chatting casually to Aston is a more straightfor-wardly comic sight, familiar to the vaudeville stage, than Davies in long underpants having his trousers flicked at him by a taunting Mick. On the other occasions, the ridiculous and vulnerable aspects of Davies are highlighted in incidents relating to his shoes and shirts (he is offered replacements) and his coat (for which substitutes such as a smoking-jacket and a caretaker's overall are offered). Characteristics of the music-hall sketch are readily discernible in the stage business and dialogue of such passages as the one where Davies first tries on a proffered pair of shoes, following an amusing and lengthy preamble from the tramp on the 'life and death' importance to him of good footwear:

ASTON. Try these.

DAVIES *takes the shoes, takes off his sandals and tries them on.*

DAVIES. Not a bad pair of shoes. (*He trudges round the room.*) They're strong all right. Yes. Not a bad shape of shoe. This leather's hardy en't? Very hardy. Some bloke tried to flog me some suede the other day. I wouldn't wear them. Can't beat leather, for wear. Suede goes off. . . . Yes. Good shoe this.
ASTON. Good.

DAVIES *waggles his feet.*

DAVIES. Don't fit though.   (p. 24)

The bathetic punch line is carefully prepared for as much by the visual effects of Davies changing footwear, pacing the room, and carefully waggling his feet as by the veritable patter act indulged in by straight-man Aston and funny-man Davies. Pinter makes less of the donning of the caretaker's white overall or velvet smoking-jacket, preferring to make the bizarre effect of the latter symbolise quite simply the character's ludicrous pretensions to sartorial elegance, much as the floral curtain material Max Miller wore – cut up into suit form! – served as an ineffable trademark of his racy outrageousness.

The silent pathetic tramp figure of the poverty-stricken Matchseller in *A Slight Ache*, unsuitably dressed for midsummer in a balaclava, muddy jumper and '*quite original*' vest (p. 192) might bring to mind the famous Charlie Chaplin persona from the silent film era. Furthermore, in his role as silent and unmoved listener to the loquacious and anxious Edward, the Matchseller may be said in the more amusing passages of the dialogue to resemble the quiet or silent stooge character favoured by popular fifties comedians such as Jimmy James or Hylda Baker – the gawky, monosyllabic idiot boy 'our Eli' and the tall vacuous truly dumb-blonde 'Cynthia'. The effects achieved by having one character, the intelligent partner in such a double act, constantly and unsuccessfully endeavouring to elicit information or a rational response from a dumb or apparently imbecilic stooge are similar to those gained by Pinter in the one-way dialogue between Edward and the Matchseller; in both the variety-hall double acts cited, the stooge's physical appearance was of paramount importance – lack of eloquence was replaced by a distinctive, ludicrous appearance which as it were spoke for itself, and helped both to keep the audience's interest and maintain the balance of theatrical impact produced by the two partners. In Pinter's hands, however, the more sinister elements of the threat of intruder upon occupier coexist with the underlying element of the comic 'double act'. Edward, the cultured and sophisticated middle-class writer, is concerned and upset by the incongruous and therefore threatening appearance of the tramp who seems to have set up a permanent pitch outside his garden:

> You look a trifle warm. Why don't you take off your balaclava? I'd find that a little itchy myself. . . .
> Do forgive me peering but is that a glass eye you're wearing? Do take off your balaclava, there's a good chap, put your tray down and take your ease, as they say in this part of the world. . . . The sweat's pouring out of you. Take off that balaclava. . . . You may think I was alarmed by the look of you. You would be quite mistaken. . . . No, no. Nothing outside this room has ever alarmed me. You disgusted me, quite forcibly, if you want to know the truth.   (pp. 185–7)

Edward's obsession with what he sees in front of him is partly built out of a desire to find out the essence of the viewed 'object', having considered its appearance; at this point in the play he is prepared to draw quick and amusing conclusions: 'You're no more disgusting than Fanny, the squire's daughter. In appearance you differ but not in essence' (p. 187).

From the silent, seemingly incompetent Matchseller who chooses the most out-of-the-way place to sell his wares Edward is doomed to receive no answer, and he feels the annoyance and the terror of not being able to pinpoint someone's true identity. Edward indulges in speculation both wild and more coolly reflective on the nagging question – to borrow Stanley Webber's phrase – of who it is he is speaking to:

> You look less and less like a cricketer the more I see of you ... God damn it, I'm entitled to know something about you! You're in my blasted house, on my territory. . . . did I . . . invite you into this room with the express intention of asking you to take off your balaclava, in order to determine your resemblance to some other person? . . . no . . . every time I have seen you you have looked quite different to the time before.   (pp. 194–7)

The incessant questioning causes Edward to collapse, since it has caused him to undertake a total re-examination of himself, his present lack of stability and peace of mind. Edward's slight ache is in his eyes, his sense of perception, and this ailment, he feels, has helped cause his downfall. 'I've caught a cold. A germ. In my eyes. . . . Not that I had any difficulty in seeing you, no, no, it was not so much my sight . . . as the airs between me and my object' (p. 198). And then, finally, following more memories of sensitively felt contact with nature and earlier schoolboy success (as a champion sprinter, like Pinter himself), Edward's last words in the play crystallise simply the unanswerable question, 'Who are you?' (p. 199). For Pinter as well as Edward, where people are concerned appearances are as deceptive and elusive as essences.

Both Davies and the Matchseller are in a sense intruder figures, ostensibly outsiders entering the society of relatively established lower-class and upper middle-class people respectively. The inspector–intruder figures of the Deadly Theatre of the provincial rep were also, as has been mentioned, distinguished by their appearance. The nearest Pinter comes to a character whose appearance denotes sinister, inquisitorial qualities is the leather-jacketed Mick in *The Caretaker*. At the time the play was written the wearing of a leather jacket would have connoted both an aggressive side to the male character and an interest in modern fashion. Mick's personality does not belie these connotations: he is a menacing character; to Davies at the end of the first act he is also a frightening intruder, a violent stalker dressed in fashionable black leather, encroaching upon what Davies has just come to regard as a secure bolt-hole. Perhaps, indeed, we are closest here, as regards Pinter's plays, to a character in sombre and sinister uniform, as stark and threatening as the MI5 man 'black from homburg to toe-cap'. In a more melodramatic context – the blind, scarred and importunate Rochester in *Jane Eyre* may be considered a relevant stimulus, unconsciously perhaps – the very appearance of Riley in *The Room*, a blind negro with a stick, helps to form in Bert Hudd's mind the image of a dangerous, ostensibly alien interloper. Despite the many dissimilarities between the two characters, both, by their appearance, produce a tension between pity and repulsion. A different kind of intruder appeared in certain rep plays Pinter acted in. This was the shabbily dressed shadowy figure from the past, usually an ex-lover, someone's skeleton in the cupboard, returned to blackmail or to make retributive or humbler demands. This person usually stood in striking contrast to the other characters, dressed in conventionally presentable attire. Rattigan's *Separate Tables*, Rhys Davies's *No Escape* and Christie's *Peril at End House* all include these figures impoverished or 'down on their luck'. In *No Man's Land* the intrusive mendicant figure of Spooner – who may or may not have been a part of Hirst's past! – is carefully set apart from the socially more secure members of the Hirst household: in his '*very old and shabby suit, dark faded shirt, creased spotted tie*' he is the polar opposite of the '*precisely dressed*' Hirst, resplendent in well-cut trousers and sports jacket, and his smartly, '*casually dressed*' servant figures, Briggs and Foster, (pp. 15, 35, 60). Spooner too has demands to make, and is self-conscious about his disadvantageous appearance: 'Let me live with you and be your secretary. . . . I ask you . . . to consider me for the post. If I were wearing a suit such as your own you would see me in a different light' (p. 88).

Where Pinter is perhaps most strikingly theatrical in his use of costume is in the business of transforming or simply altering the appearance of his characters. The dramatic precedents for transformation scenes range from Cinderella's 'rags to riches' conversion to King Lear's reversal of that process. But, more relevantly to the present work, in more modern contexts the range extends from the revelation of the disguised villain or detective to what I have termed the ugly-duckling routine, whereby a hitherto unattractive female becomes instantaneously beautiful – usually by removing spectacles and letting down her hair. In Pinter's repertory experience there were numerous examples of dramatic effects being gained in such a way. As regards the ugly-duckling routine three instances may be cited. In *Affairs of State* the plain schoolteacher Irene, whose name Louis Verneuil used as the original title to his play, is a pawn in a sophisticated political game of arranged marriages until she learns how to alter her physical appearance radically for the better. She removes spectacles and loosens hair, of course, but most importantly 'thinks beautiful'; as a result of these decisions she becomes sufficiently physically desirable to persuade the play's hero to marry her and causes the American Democratic party to rethink its strategems. Pinter played a minor role in this comedy in November 1954. Immediately after this play followed the Huddersfield production of Rosemary Casey's *Late Love*, in which Pinter played the part of a diffident bespectacled secretary to a dictatorial writer. The secretary secretly marries his employer's daughter, to the writer's extreme displeasure. Upon being challenged by his father-in-law to prove his marital suitability, the secretary ceases from nervously drying his spectacles and squares back his shoulders for the first time in the play to enable him to refer more credibly to his own manly naval background and confidently to announce the probability of his obtaining a university post in the near future. The following spring Pinter played the leading role in a sophisticated comedy, *Down Came a Blackbird*. The plot is a simple variation on the eternal-triangle theme: an attractive sensual women with little intelligence and a plain but efficient woman with an abnormally large nose vie for the hand of an eligible mature bachelor. The plain woman gains her man by wearing make-up, slimming and undergoing plastic surgery on her nose. Pinter's plays are not noted for such apparently crude and contrived transformation scenes, but when his characters undergo major transformations in physical appearance a more serious dramatic resonance is felt through being seen to be inevitable and artistically integrated rather than accidental or fanciful or contrived.

The Lover depends for much of its theatrical effectiveness on the visual impression made by the two characters' adoption of different roles, if not different personae, as they adopt different types of clothing. Richard and Sarah are first seen as conventional and rather dull middle-class people; the clothes they wear, sober suits and demure dresses, reflect their characters accurately. When they become their respective lovers, Max and Mary, they don casual seductive clothes to match their assumed personalities. Their 'disguise' clothing becomes at the end of the play as important as the 'lover' roles they adopt. Richard and Sarah begin addictively to play their Max and Mary game whilst dressed soberly:

> SARAH. . . . Why are you wearing this strange suit, and this tie? You usually wear something else, don't you? Take off your jacket. Mmmnn? Would you like me to change? Would you like me to change my clothes? I'll change for you, darling. Shall I? Would you like that?
> RICHARD. Yes. (*Pause.*) Change. (*Pause.*) Change. (*Pause.*) Change your clothes. (*Pause.*) You lovely whore.   (pp. 195–6)

The only other important transformation scene in Pinter's plays concerns the change in appearance of Stanley Webber in *The Birthday Party*. Pinter's stage directions are simple and to the point with regard to Stanley's first and last appearances in the play. At the breakfast table on the morning that Meg takes as his birthday '*he is unshaven, in his pyjamas and wears glasses*' (p. 24); following his strange re-forming treatment from Goldberg and McCann, he leaves Meg's boarding-house '*dressed in a dark well cut suit and white collar. He holds his broken glasses in his hand. He is clean-shaven*' (p. 91). The attempt violently to convert Stanley from a dishevelled, failed would-be musician into the sort of conforming human being that his smart appearance at the end of the play suggests merely reduces him to a pitiful, gibbering wreck. His true state of being belies his smart appearance, and is equivalent to that of a broken ventriloquist's dummy – his breakdown symbolised by the way he pathetically holds on to his shattered spectacles.

6 Revaluation: Movement and Dialogue

As has been noted previously, Pinter has acknowledged a fundamental concern for the visualisation of characters on a stage. Their
movements and actions are of prime importance to him:

> I find myself stuck with these characters who are either sitting or
> standing, and they've either got to walk out of a door, or come in
> through a door, and that's about all they can do.[1]

Indeed, he has spoken of the initial stimulating idea for a play in
terms principally concerning the positioning of characters:

> The germ of my plays? I'll be as accurate as I can about that. I
> went into a room and saw one person standing up and one person
> sitting down, and a few weeks later I wrote *The Room*. I went into
> another room and saw two people sitting down, and a few years
> later I wrote *The Birthday Party*. I looked through a door into a
> third room, and saw two people standing up and I wrote *The
> Caretaker*.[2]

The importance of the stage entrance or exit in Pinter's plays and
the very deliberate and significant positioning of characters at the
end of plays such as *Old Times* and *The Homecoming* have already
been noted. A character's use of a stage prop, necessarily involving
action or movement, has been similarly instanced as a significant
feature of Pinter's work. John Russell Brown, writing of these
aspects of Pinter's art, attributes them to the influence of his acting-
career:

> For Pinter, position, gesture and movement is rich in statement.
> By these essential means his characters can 'speak' without
> knowing it themselves. As an actor, Pinter knows how such
> statements are varied and controlled, and he has an 'eye' trained

96

to observe the smallest changes and potentialities. . . . in his plays he has contrived the means to make an audience 'see' this physical language for themselves. He uses posture and movement with unavoidable directness, with inventiveness, controlled complexity and, where necessary, with ambiguity.[3]

Brown cites as possible influences on Pinter the playwright Rudolf Laban, first influential in actors' schools about the time of Pinter's brief and largely unrewarding spells with RADA and the Central School, and Stanislawski's and Artaud's ideas about the importance of an actor's ability to convey meaningful movement and action. But we have noted Pinter's stated lack of interest in theory and can only conclude that his own practical experience as an actor and the close visualising of his characters whilst writing are more relevant influences on his dramatic work. Pinter's recollection of one grand effect created by gesture and movement in Wolfit's Oedipus has already been referred to:

one image of him remains with me strongly . . . he was standing high up on a rostrum with all the light on him . . . he stood with his back to the audience with a cloak round him and there came the moment when the man downstage finished his speech and we all knew, the play demanded it, the audience knew, that Wolfit or Oedipus was going to speak, was going to turn and speak.[4]

Such an effect, simple, but with a larger-than-life quality about it, was perhaps typical of the acting-style of Wolfit and McMaster. The heroic protagonists played by them were, for all important moments, upstage; downstage, watching the spectacle of the dominant kings and heroic figures were their underlings, the supporting players, and, just behind them, the audience, waiting likewise for the dramatic flourish, the awesome gesture, the impressive speech. Pinter has learned in his own way to make some of his own characters dominant in a theatrical manner when the moment calls for it. For example, Mick in *The Caretaker* reaches a point where general frustrations and the particular annoyance caused by the wheedling Davies lead him both to sever his relationship with his newly appointed caretaker and to commit a sudden act of violence. Pinter, as elsewhere in this play, places great importance on increasing the tension produced through an extended silence, by use of an actor's movement. He instructs the actor

playing Mick to stalk his prey, before calmly giving him his come-
uppance:

> DAVIES. . . . It was your brother who must have told you. He's
> nutty! . . .
>
>> MICK *walks slowly to him.*
>
> MICK. What did you call my brother?
> DAVIES. When? . . .
>
>> MICK *walks slowly round* DAVIES' *figure regarding him, once. He
>> circles him, once.*
>
> MICK. What a strange man you are. . . . It's all most regrettable
> but it looks as though I'm compelled to pay you off for your
> caretaking work. (p. 82)

Through Mick's slow encircling movement the audience and
Davies are made to experience a prolonged moment no less effective
in its own way than Wolfit's long pause followed by the turn. After
the relative calmness of the dismissal speech and the seemingly
nonchalant toss of the half-crown at Davies's feet, the climactic
moment of violence, of Mick's smashing of the Buddha, is made
more understandable and more dramatically inevitable. At the end
of the play the silent, upstage figure of Aston, still and facing the
window – his back like Wolfit's as Oedipus, turned away from the
downstage character and the audience – eloquently sums up the
finality of his separation from the man he invited to stay (pp. 86–7).
In both instances the pause – that much-used direction with which
Pinter has become almost universally associated – indicates a
stopping both of speech and action, and causes the subsequent
movement, or lack of movement in Aston's case, to make a more
dramatic impact. The former scene, of course, is not far from the
world of the thriller Pinter was so familiar with as an actor: the
inspector pacing round the suspects, the killer stalking his victim
(*The Vanity Case* and *Love from a Stranger* are examples). The latter
scene may be viewed as an unorthodox variation on the romantic
play's 'curtain' image of the two lovers or husband and wife, one
turned away, rejected (as in the endings of *Waiting for Gillian* and
Doctor Jo, in both of which the wife physically turns away from the

husband, unable to offer her love). But what is perhaps more to the point here is Pinter's awareness of what is essentially to be achieved by an actor using a given move or position to 'speak' for him. Mick's cat-and-mouse game with Davies and his cool contempt for him are given visual expression by his encircling of the tramp; Aston's quieter, determined rejection of the same character, his face resolutely turned away, crystallises his more passive kind of personality, and his different, more chilling manner of rejection, more adequately than verbal explanation.

Pinter achieves a different kind of theatrical effect – one of irony – when he allows words and actions apparently to contradict one another, thus focusing attention more powerfully upon both. Thus in *The Homecoming* the surprisingly promiscuous behaviour of Ruth, who allows herself to be intimately embraced on Max's sofa, is made to seem even more outrageous as it is accompanied by Max's conventional words of polite leave-taking to her unresponsive husband:

> MAX. . . . I'll always be glad to meet the wife. Honest. I'm telling you.
>
> > JOEY *lies heavily on* RUTH.
> > *They are almost still.*
> > LENNY *caresses her hair.*
>
> Listen, you think I don't know why you didn't tell me you were married? I know why. You were ashamed. . . . You should have known me better. I'm broadminded. I'm a broadminded man.
>
> > *He peers to see* RUTH's *face under* JOEY, *turns back to* TEDDY.
>
> Mind you, she's a lovely girl.   (p. 75)

Criticism on a narrowly realistic basis (to the effect that wives don't behave like this in front of their husbands and hosts) misses the 'surreal', 'poetic' quality of the scene, and ignores the fact that Pinter is deliberately forcing together the surface level of life and the deeper undercurrents with which the play has gradually put us in touch.

A similarly incongruous but more macabre effect is achieved at the end of *The Birthday Party*. Stanley is ushered into the room by McCann and seated on a chair by Goldberg, a pitiful zombie-like figure staring '*blankly at the floor*'. Goldberg and McCann refer to his spruce, well-dressed appearance, deliberately ignoring the fact that he is to all intents and purposes a mere shell of a human being:

> MCCANN. He looks better, doesn't he?
> GOLDBERG. Much better.
> MCCANN. A new man. . . .
>
> > *They begin to woo him, gently and with relish. During the following sequence* STANLEY *shows no reaction. He remains with no movement, where he sits.* (pp. 91–2)

The complete absence of movement indicated for Stanley here lends greater pathos to the scene, accurately defining Stanley's demotion to the rank of inert being. Pinter himself, in a letter to the first producer of *The Birthday Party*, comments on the importance of the actor in this context: 'A great deal, it seems to me, will depend on the actor. If he copes with Stanley's loss of himself successfully, I believe a certain amount of poignancy will emanate.'[5]

In addition, the lack of movement on Stanley's part affords greater effectiveness to the subsequent subtle movements given to Stanley when he attempts to answer the questions of his interrogators:

> GOLDBERG. Well, Stanny boy, what do you say, eh?
>
> > *They watch. He concentrates. His head lowers, his chin draws into his chest, he crouches.*
>
> STANLEY. Ug-gughh ... uh-gughhh. . . .
> MCCANN. What's your opinion of the prospect?
>
> > STANLEY'*s body shudders, relaxes, his head drops, he becomes still again, stooped.* (pp. 94–5)

Stanley's inability to talk or move to any effect tells us emphatically of his shattered condition, his state of being. As elsewhere in Pinter what matters is not so much what is said or done, but whether a character is talking or not, moving or remaining still. Again, in this particular case, Pinter has made a significant comment on the importance of the passage in relation to the identity of the character:

> Stanley *cannot* perceive his only valid justification – which is he is what he is – therefore he certainly can never be articulate about it. . . . In the rattle in his throat Stanley approximates nearer to the true nature of himself than ever before and certainly ever after.[6]

One character's position relative to another is time and again in Pinter accurately representative of the relationship – whether of dominance or subservience – between them. Stanley Webber's refusal to sit down during his first meeting with Goldberg and McCann is highlighted in a richly comic sequence. Sitting down is seen by the interrogators as a natural and necessary prerequisite of being interrogated. Sitting and standing take on ludicrous but menacing symbolic connotations in a sequence on one level more reminiscent of the music-hall knockabout act than of anything else:

GOLDBERG. Sit down.
STANLEY. No.

> GOLDBERG *sighs, and sits at the table right.*

GOLDBERG. McCann.
MCCANN. Nat?
GOLDBERG. Ask him to sit down.
MCCANN. Yes, Nat. (MCCANN *moves to* STANLEY.) Do you mind sitting down?
STANLEY. Yes, I do mind.
MCCANN. Yes, now, but – it'd be better if you did. . . .
MCCANN. All right. If you will I will.

> MCCANN *slowly sits at the table, left.*

MCCANN. Well?
STANLEY. Right. Now you've both had a rest you can get out!
MCCANN (*rising*). That's a dirty trick! I'll kick the shite out of him!
GOLDBERG (*rising*). No! I have stood up.
MCCANN. Sit down again.

GOLDBERG. Once I'm up I'm up.
STANLEY. Same here.   (pp. 56–7)

Sitting down is seen here, all but consciously by the characters concerned, as being synonymous with compliance; standing, on the contrary, is the position to be adopted by those with 'business' to do. When the first interrogation really gets under way, Stanley is seen first clutching and bending over a chair with his questioners standing either side of it; then the next two stage directions indicate that Stanley turns and sits with his back to the audience. The stage direction is an unusual one. In effect the audience can relate more to the character as he undergoes relentless interrogation facing the same way as they. The position, though an uncommon one in the theatre, was not unfamiliar to Pinter. As David Baron he played the title role in Mary Hayley Bell's *The Uninvited Guest* whilst at Colchester. The play includes an interrogation scene that was mentioned in the local review:

> David Baron . . . keeps our interest very effectively and fully exploits the mystery and strangeness of the part [a person released from a mental asylum]. It is a good idea to have him stand with his back to the audience while other characters question him; and by other devices he conveys well the movements and attitude of a man who has been set free after being imprisoned in this way. [7]

The 'mystery and strangeness' of Goldberg and McCann's bizarre questioning is enhanced by such use of an unusual stage direction. Stanley has his back to the wall, and, as the audience is in a sense the fourth wall of the proscenium stage, it is in effect more involved: it both receives Goldberg and McCann's questions more directly, owing to the interrogators' stage position, and represents an immediate and final barrier, cutting off any possible way of escape for Stanley.

There are two other instances where the simple matter of sitting or not sitting down is used to considerable dramatic effect. Ruth in *The Homecoming* asks her husband for a seat on their arrival at his family home:

> RUTH. Can I sit down?
> TEDDY. Of course.
> RUTH. I'm tired.

Pause.

TEDDY. Then sit down.

She does not move. (p. 36)

Ruth's decision not to follow her husband's obvious advice points to a more general refusal on her part to oblige Teddy. It contributes to the 'edginess' of the situation, to the sense the audience quickly receives of a lack of ease between them, and indicates Ruth's uncertainty about whether she has done right to accompany her husband on this visit to his family home. In fact the play – with its final image of Ruth as matriarch sitting relaxed in Max's chair, here originally proffered her by Teddy – may eventually be seen as *her* homecoming. Similarly, in the opening of *The Caretaker* a kind of tension is created through the tramp's prolonged hesitation before accepting the repeated offer of a seat by his new-found host, Aston. Here the standard invitation to sit in itself calls for dramatic action in relation to the disposition of the set:

ASTON. Sit down.
DAVIES. Thanks (*looking about*). Uuh ...
ASTON. Just a minute.

> ASTON *looks around for a chair, sees one lying on its side by the rolled carpet on the fireplace, and starts to get it out.*

DAVIES. Sit down? Huh ... I haven't had a good sit down ... I haven't had a proper sit down ... well, I couldn't tell you ...
ASTON. (*placing the chair*). Here you are. (pp. 16–17)

But it is several minutes before Davies, though earnestly requiring rest, will allow himself to sit down, and the audience is provoked into seeking the reasons why – his mistrustfulness, his suspicion of kindness all too rarely offered him, his pride and the restlessness connected with his narrow escape from being 'done in down there'. Only when he has talked out his explanation of the 'commotion' (pp. 17, 19) he has just been involved in can he finally relax enough to sit down, and then thank Aston, his rescuer, for his help. As an addendum to these points on the special significance Pinter often attaches to a character's sitting or not sitting, *Landscape* may be specially cited as a play in which all the 'action' is reduced to two people sitting *'relaxed, in no sense rigid'* in an armchair and ordinary chair of a country-house kitchen, recollecting emotions in the relative tranquillity of their sedentary position. But the audience would be misled if it accepted such a simple symbolical explanation for the characters' uninterrupted sitting. The audience has much to do to interpret the 'meaning' of a play – a play of reflection, inaction, pause and silence – in which the characters appear at no time to achieve a direct, unequivocal communication, since neither appears to hear the other's voice, as the author indicates in his introductory note. Peter Davison has recognised that a special responsibility rests with any audience of *Landscape*: for the play to succeed, ambiguities about the dialogue (and, I suggest, the question of lack of stage movement) must be met by the minds of the people watching the actors perform. Peter Davison sees a link between the audience's involvement in *Landscape* (and *Silence*) and an audience's response to a music hall comedian: 'These plays are remarkable dramatic and theatrical experiences which make the most subtle use of the well-tried music-hall technique of innuendo.'[8] The 'work' the audience has to do to interpret the ambiguities of meaning and emotional significance in the gaps between the lines in Pinter's dialogue resembles the filling-in of the innuendoes or double meanings suggested by a music-hall comic, who will pause for such theatrical interaction to occur. I should like to add that, depending on the manner of production, various other elements of the music-hall tradition may be found in *Landscape* and *Silence*, especially in passages where attention is directly or indirectly drawn to the sedentary posture of the characters. Take Beth and Duff in *Landscape* on their separate verbal journeys – the former constantly reminiscing, the latter intermittently trying to communicate:

> BETH. They all held my arm lightly, as I stepped out of the car, or out of the door, or down the steps. Without exception. If they touched the back of my neck, or my hand, it was done so lightly. Without exception. With one exception.
>
> DUFF. Mind you, there was a lot of shit all over the place, all along the paths, by the pond. Dogshit, duckshit ... all kinds of shit ... all over the paths. The rain didn't clean it up. It made it even more treacherous.
>
> *Pause.*

The ducks were well away, right over on their island. But I wouldn't have fed them anyway. I would have fed the sparrows.

BETH. I could stand now. I could be the same. I dress differently, but I am beautiful.

Silence.

DUFF. You should have a walk with me one day down to the pond, bring some bread. There's nothing to stop you.

Pause. (p. 180.)

Besides its poignant qualities, stemming from the emotional gulf between the two, and the nostalgic delusions of Beth, the scene has comic potential. First, there is the contrast between straight man and funny man, with traditional lack of communication and different modes of address – one gently and pathetically repetitive and poetic, the other cacophonously and comically repetitive and down-to-earth; and, secondly, there is the possibility of a wry, amused response by the audience to the lack of action following each attempt at 'getting somewhere' or progressing. This culminates in Beth's literally getting or going nowhere following her brave attempt to change her present stagnant immobility and transform it into the vibrancy of her past: 'I could stand now. I could be the same [as I was!]' – but she is unable to move, to change, even though there is, at least in Duff's mind, nothing to stop her! One is surely not far, here, from the pathetic/comic position of Beckett's Vladimir and Estragon (in their turn possessing recognised music-hall traits) at the end of *Waiting for Godot*, which sees both determined to go (and thus go on in life) but neither willing to make a move.

Silence, where sitting again predominates, takes its title partly, it seems to me, from the lack of any real communication between the three characters, but also from the mysterious but crucial speech of Ellen:

Around me sits the night. Such a silence. I can hear myself. Cup my ear. My heart beats in my ear. Such a silence. Is it me? Am I silent or speaking? How can I know? Can I know such things? No one has ever told me. I need to be told things. I seem to be old.

Am I old now? No one will tell me. I must find a person to tell me these things. (p. 211.)

These lines seem eerily to foreshadow the predicament of the heroine of *A Kind of Alaska* (1982), for whom time has remained static for twenty-five years during her peculiarly chronic sleeping-sickness. It is as if time and space sit rather than stand still for Ellen; perhaps she has picked up the idea from Rumsey, who five minutes previously – after a break in the text denoted as '*Silence*' – has remarked, 'It is curiously hot. Sitting weather I call it. The weather sits, does not move. Unusual' (p. 207). Thus the symbolic importance of characters sitting in *Silence*, and thus continuing to reflect, not to change, not to progress in their relationships, but to dwell on what has been and what might have been, is reflected in the peculiarity of their present time-setting, which aptly gives every indication of being unchanging.

When characters fall down or lie down in Pinter's plays there is usually a more than normal theatrical and symbolic effectiveness present. Often a more metaphorical downfall, permanent or temporary, is implied. The pathetic drunken figure of Hirst in *No Man's Land* crawling on all fours (see p. 67) is the vividly realised image of a man in despair, drinking himself to a paralytic, nerveless stupor, towards his no man's land, icy and silent. In the earlier play *The Collection* much is made of the accidental fall of one of the characters. In the sequence the acts of lying down, standing or sitting are again given more than usual significance. James may or may not have been cuckolded by Bill, and has been questioning him about the possibility. Bill, of course, is keen to get rid of his inquiring visitor; James makes a '*sudden move forward*' after receiving Bill's friendly invitation to leave, and causes Bill to start back and fall '*over a pouffe on to the floor*'. The positions of dominance and subservience are thus graphically reversed, since James first chuckles then '*stands over him*', refusing to answer Bill's immediate requests to be allowed to rise. James exacts every amount of pressure he can from his literally superior position and the matter of the possible cuckolding is opened up again:

BILL. . . . If you let me get up ... I'll ... I'll tell you ... the truth ...

Pause.

JAMES. Tell me the truth from there.

Pause.

BILL. No. No, when I'm up.
JAMES. Tell me from there.

Pause.

BILL. Oh well. I'm only telling you because I'm utterly bored . . . . (pp. 135–6.)

The two characters then argue about the supposed hotel incident in Leeds involving Bill and James's wife Stella. Physical positions again assume prime importance!

JAMES. . . . She didn't have much to say. You were sitting on the bed, next to her.

Silence.

BILL. Not sitting. Lying.

BLACKOUT (p. 137)

Sam's fall at the end of *The Homecoming* may at first glance appear merely melodramatic, a theatrical moment contrived for its own sake. The last scene has apparently reached a peaceful conclusion with Ruth coming to terms in more than one sense with Max, Joey and Lenny and her husband Teddy: her responsibilities as new mother of the family are being designated calmly and efficiently when Sam makes his dramatic outburst:

RUTH. Well, it might prove a workable arrangement.
LENNY. I think so.
MAX. And you'd have the whole of your daytime free.
LENNY. Make the beds.
MAX. Scrub the place out a bit.
TEDDY. Keep everyone company.

SAM *comes forward.*

SAM (*in one breath*). MacGregor had Jessie in the back of my cab as I drove them along.

> *He croaks and collapses.*
> *He lies still.*
> *They look at him.* (pp. 93–4)

Like Ruth before him, however, Sam is using the act of lying on the floor to his own advantage. He may at first sight appear to be either dead or dying, and Max and the family callously argue about these possibilities, but Pinter, in an interview, assures us, 'He doesn't die. Actually, he's in fine form',[9] and this we can verify by closer examination of the text: Sam has made his point, disapproving of what he sees as Max's manipulation of a woman with children to look after ('Don't be silly. . . . She's got three children' – p. 86), but he lacks the moral fibre to fight the case, and, like Teddy, opts out of the matter. His lying-low may be seen here, therefore, not as a result of a heart attack, melodramatically introduced by the author, but as an indication of the character's cowardice, his final non-involvement with an argument, an escape from any possible retribution from Max. Another fall that on a superficial view might seem melodramatic and contrived is that of Edward in *A Slight Ache*. This play, originally written for the radio, has many surreal touches, and the combination of Edward's physical collapse and his continuing to expatiate, from the floor, on past successes and present insecurities seems at the least bizarre. The fall, in fact, may only be seen as a successful move on Pinter's part if it is looked at in a symbolic light: Edward's breakdown, his loss of confidence, is highlighted by his loss of upright posture. The Matchseller's role becomes the dominant one when he gets up from his seat, an act which brings about a long pause or '*Silence*', as Pinter indicates, and causes Edward voice his fear of being superseded by a younger man: 'You look younger. You look extraordinarily ... youthful ... licked men twice my strength ... when a stripling ... like yourself' (p. 199). Edward's unease, incidentally, had begun with a statement that significantly stresses the dramatic importance of posture or physical stance:

> No listen, let me be quite frank with you shall I? I really cannot understand why you don't sit down. There are four chairs at your disposal. . . . I can't possibly talk to you unless you're settled.

Then and only then can I speak to you. . . . (*Pause.*) . . . Go into
the corner then. Into the corner. Go on. Get into the shade of the
corner. Back. Backward. . . . Ah, you understand me. Forgive
me for saying so, but I had decided that you had the comprehen-
sion of a bullock.   (p. 186)

From the comments of actors quoted at the beginning of this study
(see p. 2) it may be seen that Pinter's use of language in the plays is
popular with the people who have to give voice to it on the stage.
The matter is partly one of fluency: the lines are eminently
'speakable', being for the most part a pastiche of everyday speech
patterns. Pinter's ear for the rhythms of contemporary spoken
English in its different registers is generally acknowledged, as is his
ability to write in such a way that 'the words really do come off the
tongue and teeth beautifully'. Witness, for example, the fluency
apparent in the most prosaic of speeches. Here is Mrs Sands, a minor
character from Pinter's first play, *The Room*:

Yes, Mrs Hudd, you see, the thing is, Mrs Hudd, we'd heard
they'd got a room to let here, so we thought we'd come along and
have a look. Because we're looking for a place, you see,
somewhere quiet, and we knew this district was quiet, and we
passed the house a few months ago and we thought it looked very
nice, but we thought we'd call of an evening, to catch the
landlord, so we came along this evening.   (pp. 116–17)

The actress playing Mrs Sands would be able to pick up the
repetitive rhythms of a working-class London woman's speech. She
would have little trouble in finding a 'character' through which to
project Mrs Sands, just as she would not find the phrasing and
stressing of the speech at all difficult, since this passage like so many
others in Pinter is an accurate representation of the spoken language
used by contemporary people. At first read-through the speech
appears most inelegant, monotonous and prolix, but it affords the
actress many opportunities to make the piece vibrant and richly
comic. And a close examination of the speech well bears out Dennis
Welland's statement on the special nature of Pinter's linguistic skill:
'the rhythms of speech, repetitive or varying, fluid or staccato, can
often communicate more than the prose meanings of the constituent
words'.[10]
The newly arrived would-be tenants, Mr and Mrs Sands, have

been bickering in an excessively childish and indulgent way, and
Mrs Sands is brought to her senses by Rose's pertinent question,
'You say you saw a man downstairs, in the basement?' (p. 116). The
repetition of the phrases, 'you see', 'Mrs Hudd', 'we thought', and
the reiterated blandishment about needing a 'quiet' place will not,
when uttered by an actress of reasonable ability, add up to a flat,
unimaginative droning-on, but should reflect both a woman's
precise and insistent attempts to explain the reasons for her present
action and exaggerated stabs at regaining credibility and approval.
The rhythms of the speech are fluid both at the beginning and at the
end, where Mrs Sands's gently confident and reassuring remarks are
couched in cadences both following the consequential conjunction
'so'; the phrases and clauses in the main body of the passage are of a
more staccato nature, with the repeated use of the simple additional
conjunction, and reflect the difficulties faced by the speaker as she
tries to compress a whole history of recent deliberations and
decisions made by her husband and herself – at least, allegedly by
both of them! Thus, the representation of a woman striving,
relatively successfully, to project an image of unflurried plausibility
is realised by this carefully worked stylisation of natural speech.
Beyond this, the sense of mystery and ambiguity in Pinter's plays
gives considerable scope to the actor. Sir Ralph Richardson speaks
of his feelings about playing in *No Man's Land*:

> There isn't any plot. But that never bothers an actor. And the
> characters are never really rounded off. They don't quite know
> who they are. But that's rather natural in a way. We don't know
> exactly who we are, do we? We hardly know anybody else, really
> completely. . . . We're a mystery to ourselves, and to other
> people. [11]

The ambiguities and ambivalences of people in the real world are
present in the characters Pinter creates. The actions they perform
and the words they use offer clues but no definite answers. Yet
precisely because of this ambiguity the characters remain vibrantly
alive for actors to play:

> [*The Homecoming*] certainly means more to me now than when we
> rehearsed it, when I first read it. Pinter is throwing things open.
> All I understand about the play is that it is an actor's dream. And
> I'm sure Lenny's speech about a night on the waterfront will be

an actor's audition speech from now until the end of time. It's such a joy to play and I think it's very open. It's a very full play and you could read virtually anything about life into it.[12]

Here John Normington, of the original cast of Peter Hall's and Pinter's joint production of *The Homecoming*, hints at the opportunity to help in creating a role; the challenge to the Pinter player seems to be more than the normal interpretative one. Paul Rogers, from the same cast, is perhaps more lucid on this point, namely the sense of greater responsibility that is afforded the actor in a Pinter play – even in one which Pinter is codirecting:

> Pinter will not interfere. You can ask him, but you will have to beg him for information. He's always fascinated by the possibilities of writer–actor–audience relationships. He's not going to allow anything to come between reactions within the triumvirate.[13]

The ambiguities and difficulties of characterisation stem mostly from lack of definite information (as regards exposition or motivation) given in the text. Sometimes it is artistically advisable to keep interpretative options open, not to spoil textual ambiguities by opting definitely for one reading rather than another. John Normington, who played the relatively minor character of Sam in *The Homecoming*, makes an interesting comment on this facet of 'playing' Pinter:

> Before I did *The Homecoming*, I thought it was necessary to Sell with a capital s. That you must really come on, make it absolutely clear what you are doing. This taught me how much the audience will come to you. They get far more involved if they're wondering why he's doing that or what he's going to be. . . . Finally it was a great help that the text was economical, but it didn't help me initially. . . . It didn't hit me until the middle of the rehearsals that the text would help me to give a very understated performance.[14]

Paul Rogers – Max in the first production of *The Homecoming* – gets to the heart of this matter of allowing the ambiguity of a speech to exist in performance. In the interview with John Lahr, Rogers discusses the significance of Max's strange confrontation with

Teddy after grossly insulting his wife and savagely attacking two other members of the family:

> INTERVIEWER. At the end of the first act you begin to square off. Now this is a kind of ritual battle isn't it?
>
> ROGERS. Oh, but it isn't a question of fighting. . . . No. You remember that the invitation was to give his old father a kiss and a cuddle. And at the end of the act, they're absolutely four square with each other and Teddy says, 'Come on, Dad, I'm ready for the cuddle'. And it means cuddle. It doesn't mean I'll knock your block off. It means I *could* knock your block off, you silly old bastard. There is an ambiguity there, as with every word they utter. Max brings the curtain down with a roar of delight and triumph: 'He still loves his father!' And he does.[15]

Obviously a great deal of attention needs to be paid to subtext by the Pinter player. Awareness of ambiguities in the text can come only after much reading 'between' or 'behind' the lines, and for the actor to function at all certain decisions about the past lives of the characters have to be made. These decisions are of course harder to make given Pinter's special linguistic concern with verbal stratagems, with contradictions in a text terser and more economical than most. Paul Rogers, for example, found it necessary to grasp Max's present and past attitudes towards a character, MacGregor, who does not actually take part in the play. MacGregor, it is stated, had sex with Max's wife, Jessie. John Lahr asked Paul Rogers whether he felt he, as Max, was hurt by Jessie; Rogers replies, 'Not by Jessie, by MacGregor. And yet MacGregor was forgiven because MacGregor was his friend. It was almost the Eskimo attitude. MacGregor is still the friend, but behind there is the bitterness of betrayal.'[16]

A related aspect of Pinter's plays to which the actor necessarily responds is the way in which, out of the linguistic games and the struggles, now comic, now sinister, to map out relationships, the matter of role-playing assumes a key importance. An actor is necessarily a role-player, and this fact in itself may lead to some confusion of identity. The task of being required to assume professionally many different roles may have an effect on the actor's own sense of himself. Pinter himself has admitted, 'I often look at myself in the mirror and say who the hell's that?'[17] Ralph Richardson has something similar to say: 'The trouble is I can never remember who I am whenever I'm photographed. Who *am* I? I find I'm no one in particular'.[18] A similar fluidity of approach to identity has been adopted by Pinter in respect of his approach to the creating of characters. Characters, he insists, are not fixed and 'given' but open to negotiation:

> The relationship between author and characters should be a highly respectful one, both ways. . . . You arrange *and* you listen, following the clues you leave for yourself, through the characters. And sometimes a balance is found, where image can freely engender image and where at the same time you are able to keep your sights on the place where the characters are silent and in hiding.[19]

And the language of the plays offers many examples of a reality negotiated through dialogue between characters, through verbal stratagems and the adoption of different personae. In rehearsal, as well as in performance, an actor may be said to be indulging in an ever-changing negotiation between himself and the text in interpreting the character he is being asked to play.

The concepts of role-playing and negotiating character and identity are fundamental to *The Lover*. That Richard and Sarah play at being each other's lover when they are not assuming their normal roles of husband and wife may seem at first glance a mere actor's exercise, a delightful game for actors to indulge themselves in. This is of course the dangerously fallacious critical stance taken by Nigel Dennis and others. It can be refuted only by closer examination of the text, which may reveal an underlying seriousness in the relationship between the author and his characters and between the characters in their exploration of their own complex relationship. When Richard and Sarah adopt their pretend roles of lover, they not only assume different names but in fact try on different personae, various roles of sensualist, dirty old man, virgin, whore and others. As a married couple they like to score points off one another in games relating to different levels of pretence and in more serious attempts to disturb or gain ascendancy over the other. At the beginning of the play only Sarah admits to having a lover; Richard is then accused by Sarah of having a mistress. Richard has apparently not been accused in a similar manner before ('You've never put it to me so bluntly before, have you?') and retorts in a fashion that reduces Sarah's adopted role from mistress to whore.

Sarah, as far as one can gather from her questions and the pauses for thought, is taken aback, arguably hurt:

> SARAH. I must say I never expected you to admit to it so readily.
> RICHARD. Oh, why not? You've never put it to me so bluntly before, have you? Frankness at all costs. Essential to a healthy marriage. Don't you agree?
> SARAH. Of course. (p. 168)

Pinter exploits all the tensions involved in the strange 'double-think' kind of frankness adopted by the pair, who by the end of the play seem too inextricably trapped in their world of make-believe to be considered partners in a 'healthy marriage'. Richard attempts to get rid of 'Max' and the whore figure that Sarah has been playing. Sarah is most disturbed by this severe tampering with the agreed rules of the game, and is eventually moved to strike back by claiming other lovers. Examination of the possible truth of this claim is precluded by Richard's adoption of the role of Max, to the delight of both parties (pp. 189–94). Thus in a very graphic way Pinter reveals a particular concern of his with the theme of avoidance of communication and the verbal means people adopt to secure this end.[20]

Richard and Sarah share with Deeley in *Old Times*, Spooner in *No Man's Land* and, to a limited extent, Ben and Gus in *The Dumb Waiter* both the ability to assume different roles and a tendency to step back from a conversation and comment on the language being used in it. Occasionally the effect is a slightly alienating one: the audience is all but addressed by the speaker, or at least is, as it were, invited to move closer into the conversation. In the dialogue between Richard and Sarah one is occasionally reminded of the criticism uttered by Gwendolen Fairfax in Wilde's *The Importance of Being Earnest*: 'In matters of grave importance style, not sincerity, is the vital thing.'[21] Richard talks of being delighted 'To hear your command of contemporary phraseology, your delicate use of the very latest idiomatic expression, so subtly employed' (p. 187). Previously Sarah, in her normal role of wife, comments on Richard's tendency to sound rather pretentious in his descriptions of their complicated views on sexual relations:

> RICHARD. . . . If I, for instance, were called upon to fulfil the function of a lover and felt disposed, shall we say, to accept the

> job, well, I'd as soon give it up as be found incapable of
> executing its proper and consistent obligation.
> SARAH. You do use long words.
> RICHARD. Would you prefer me to use short ones?
> SARAH. No, thank you. (pp. 186–7)

The alternative of 'four-letter' words is unacceptable to Sarah in
this context of husband talking to wife; in the context of lover to
mistress/whore a different mode of language is used:

> SARAH. You men are all alike. Give me a cigarette.
> RICHARD. I bloody well won't.
> SARAH. I beg your pardon?
> RICHARD. Come here, Dolores. (p. 178)

Deeley, like Spooner after him, is another example of a character
who with varying degrees of success uses language as a weapon of
defence or attack, or as a means of obtaining a more secure foothold
in a relationship. Deeley may be less successful than either Richard
or Spooner as a linguistic manipulator of people, but he has a verbal
buoyancy which he uses to keep his head above water in his dealings
with Kate and Anna. Towards the end of the play he feels subtly
intimidated by both women and adopts at one stage a colloquial
casualness, using a mixture of sixties hippy slang and the snappy
irreverent colloquialisms of a Max Miller telling his 'clean' dirty
stories (see p. 74):

> We've met before, you know. Anna and I .... Yes, we met in
> the Wayfarers Tavern. In the corner. She took a fancy to me. Of
> course I was slim-hipped in those days. Pretty nifty. A bit
> squinky, quite honestly. Curly hair. The lot. We had a scene
> together. She freaked out. She didn't have any bread, so I bought
> her a drink. She looked at me with big eyes, shy, all that bit. She
> was pretending to be you at the time. Did it pretty well. Wearing
> your underwear she was too, at the time. Amiably allowed me a
> gander. Trueblue generosity. Admirable in a woman. (p. 69)

At more exasperated moments Deeley flippantly adopts identities
which he dismisses as easily as the putting on and off of an
impressionist–comedian's silly hat:

I had a great crew in Sicily. A marvellous cameraman. Irving
Shultz. Best in the business. We took a pretty austere look at the
women in black. The little old women in black. I wrote the film
and directed it. My name is Orson Welles. . . . As a matter of
fact, I am at the top of my profession as a matter of fact, and I
have indeed been associated with substantial numbers of articu-
late and sensitive people, mainly prostitutes of all kinds.   (p. 42)

In Act I he is occasionally provoked by Anna's use of idiom, which
he finds false or possibly affected. Language for him is a clear
indication of character. Deeley is made uncomfortable by Anna's
talk of her luxurious Mediterranean lifestyle. He immediately
adopts a flippant approach to the conversation and switches
personae from pedant to deliberately polite small-talker, and finally
to cheerful working-class host figure:

My work took me to Sicily. My work concerns itself with life all
over, you see, in every part of the globe. With people all over the
globe. I use the word globe because the word world possesses
emotional political sociological and psychological pretentions
and resonances which I prefer as a matter of choice to do without,
or shall I say to steer clear of, or if you like to reject. How's the
yacht?

ANNA. Oh, very well.
DEELEY. Captain steer a straight course?
ANNA. As straight as we wish, when we wish it.
DEELEY. Don't you find England damp, returning?
ANNA. Rather beguilingly so.
DEELEY. Rather beguilingly so? (*To himself.*) What the hell does
   she mean by that? . . . Well, any time your husband finds
   himself in this direction my little wife will be only too glad to
   put the old pot on the old gas stove and dish him up something
   luscious if not voluptuous. No trouble.   (pp. 40–1)

Spooner in *No Man's Land* tries more sophisticated kinds of verbal
dexterity in order to gain favour and employment from his
unwilling host. Although early in the play he is given to sudden
aggressively playful denigrations of Hirst (see p. 67), mainly his
delivery is of a more refined and elegant variety. At times Pinter
gives him the casual sophistication of a character from a play by

Oscar Wilde. (Again one is reminded, as with Richard in *The Lover*, of Gwendolen Fairfax's remark on style and sincerity.) It is in the elegance of style, and the coolness and self-possession with which he asserts unconventional attitudes, that Pinter's character approaches a typical Wildean one:

> My only security, you see, my true comfort and solace, rests in the confirmation that I elicit from people of all kinds a common and constant level of indifference. . . . To show interest in me or, good gracious, anything tending towards a positive liking of me would cause in me a condition of the acutest alarm. (p. 17)

Spooner cannot resist the temptation to go over the top, to play the ham actor, as it were, as when, towards the end of the play, he delivers a most flowery verbal *curriculum vitae* with extravagant promises of fine future service to Hirst:

> I will accept death's challenge on your behalf. I shall meet it for your sake, boldly, whether it be in the field or in the bedchamber. I am your Chevalier. I had rather bury myself in a tomb of honour than permit your dignity to be sullied by domestic enemy or foreign foe. (p. 89)

If this role is unsuitably 'heroic' Spooner obligingly offers a more low-key and down to earth one: 'Before you reply, I would like to say one thing more. I occasionally organise poetry readings, in the upstairs room of a particular public house' (p. 90).

As a writer Spooner is capable of playing the role of linguistic critic and drawing the audience's attention directly to the script, as when he humorously mocks Hirst's reluctance to talk:

> SPOONER. . . . All we have left is the English language. Can it be salvaged? That is my question.
> HIRST. You mean in what rests its salvation?
> SPOONER. More or less.
> HIRST. Its salvation must rest in you.
> SPOONER. It's uncommonly kind of you to say so. In you too, perhaps, although I haven't sufficient evidence to go on. (pp. 18–19)

The play's first audiences thoroughly appreciated the humour of

John Gielgud's way of delivering the last sentence almost as an aside to the audience, as if this were a rather sophisticated version of a music-hall double-act. Spooner steps out of the role of conversationalist into the role of linguistic commentator in the previously mentioned exchange before Hirst's collapse:

> HIRST. Tonight ... my friend ... you find me in the last lap of a race ... I had long forgotten to run.
>
> *Pause.*
>
> SPOONER. A metaphor. Things are looking up.   (p. 32)

Closer to the world of the two-man comedy act are, of course, Ben and Gus from *The Dumb Waiter*, who in their own manner treat the language they use as itself a point of discussion or altercation:

> GUS. How can you light a kettle?
> BEN. It's a figure of speech.
> GUS. I've never heard it.
> BEN. Light the kettle! It's common usage.   (p. 141)

Peter Davison has convincingly shown this sequence to be derived from the kind of worldplay indulged in by Flanagan and Allen:

> FLANAGAN. Anyway, I lied the hole wertical.
> ALLEN.   What?
> FLANAGAN. I lied it — wertical.
> ALLEN. *Lied* it?!
> FLANAGAN. Laided it.
> ALLEN. You laid it.
> FLANAGAN. Yes, neuter gender, laided it.[22]

The Flanagan and Allen routine reaches zany heights of nonsense indulged in for its own sake, as well as reflecting the nature of the relationship between 'crazy' Flanagan and 'sensible' Allen. Likewise, Gus and Ben seem to be carrying their linguistic argument to ludicrous extremes, but it is explicitly seen as an argument which focuses our attention on the shakiness of the professional relationship between the two gunmen:

GUS. I bet my mother used to say it.
BEN. Your mother? When did you last see your mother?
GUS. I don't know, about –
BEN. Well what are you talking about your mother for?

They stare.

Gus, I'm not trying to be unreasonable. I'm just trying to point something out to you.
GUS. Yes, but –
BEN. Who's the senior partner here, me or you?
GUS. You.
BEN. I'm only looking after your interests, Gus. . . . Nobody says light the gas!   (p. 142)

Austin Quigley's statement about this passage in particular and Pinter dialogue in general is a pertinent summing-up of the importance of the role of language in Pinter's plays: 'The point to be grasped about the verbal activity in a Pinter play is that language is not so much a means of referring to structure in personal relationships as a means of creating it.'[23]

These verbal manipulators in Pinter's plays may be seen as 'good actors', to use Katharine Worth's term.[24] She uses the phrase to denote those Pinter characters 'who can project an identity with panache'. From this description of characters in the plays the tendency for actors to enjoy playing role-players becomes even more understandable. The loquacious story-tellers and poseurs of the plays are perhaps the most immediately attractive roles for actors to play. Amongst them we may consider Max and Lenny in *The Homecoming*, Mick in *The Caretaker* and Goldberg and Stanley in *The Birthday Party*.

Lenny's sexually suggestive talk to Ruth has often been commented on as a brilliant example of freewheeling bluff – the story of the experience by the docks with the prostitute, complete with crude colloquialisms such as 'falling apart with the pox' and stand-up comedians' humorous bits of padding: 'watching all the steamers steaming up, no one about, all quiet on the Western Front' is a recognisable mask of macho pretension, which is, however, unsuccessful in putting down Ruth (pp. 46–7). Equally marked and rather more successful in terms of putting down the 'victim' is Lenny's later assumption of the mask of philosopher complete with relevant jargon:

LENNY. . . . Eh, Teddy, you haven't told us much about your Doctorship of Philosophy. What do you teach?

TEDDY. Philosophy.

LENNY. Well, I want to ask you something. Do you detect a certain logical incoherence in the central affirmations of Christian theism?

TEDDY. That question doesn't fall within my province.   (p. 67)

Similarly, in *The Caretaker* Mick's aggressive instincts are given voice often under an assumed role (see p. 45). Mick's common trick of using the technical jargon of the furniture business ('a table in afromosia teak veneer, an armchair in oatmeal tweed' – p. 81) and the legal and insurance professions ('benefit extension, compensation on cessation, comprehensive indemnity against Riot, Civil Commotion, Labour Disturbances, Storm, Tempest, Thunderbolt, Larceny or Cattle' – p. 45) has been noted as a weapon he uses to impress and frighten the ignorant intruder, Davies. It is also an indication of Mick's pretensions to a station in life higher than his lowly one of van-driver. The verbal games of Max in *The Homecoming* are subtler. As Paul Rogers has pointed out, they are characterised by double-meaning, a two-way manifestation of love and hatred.[25] This explains the macabre quality of such a speech as 'Look, next time you come over, don't forget to let us know beforehand whether you're married or not. I'll always be glad to meet the wife' (p. 75) – uttered calmly whilst Ruth is being fondled by Lenny and Joey; or of the hostile welcome given to Teddy and Ruth: 'I haven't seen the bitch for six years, he comes home without a word, he brings a filthy scrubber off the street, he shacks up in my house!' (p. 58). This is more readily understandable if one bears in mind Paul Rogers's view of Max's attack as a gambit:

> This is my opening attack on Teddy. She [Ruth] is a means to an end. I don't know where she comes from, I don't know what kind of a girl she is. *Max is only interested in how Teddy will respond.* It's my big attack on him for treating me and the family in the way that he has.[26]

The whole cast of *The Homecoming* are seen by Rogers as playing games of daring with each other – games of cruelty stemming from thwarted love, a kind of perverse sublimation of the more conventional, charitable family feeling.

The Birthday Party's two main characters, Stanley and Goldberg, have their talkative, role-playing extrovert natures constantly on show. Both in their different ways are in part reminiscent of comic figures of the illegitimate theatre. Goldberg as 'stage-Jewish' caricature has already been linked with the verbally expansive figure of Anew McMaster, and with the menacing intruder figures of the detective play. The ribald stand-up music-hall comic is also a constituent part of this character; undertones of Max Miller or even Groucho Marx (both, as noted previously, favourite comedians of Pinter) are, it seems to me, present in the exchange with Lulu on the morning after the night before:

GOLDBERG. Come over here.

LULU. No, thank you.

GOLDBERG. What's the matter? You got the needle to Uncle Natey? . . . Have a game of pontoon first, for old time's sake.

LULU. I've had enough games.

GOLDBERG. A girl like you, at your age, at your time of health, and you don't take to games? . . .

LULU. . . . . what would Eddie say? . . . He didn't come into my room at night with a briefcase!

GOLDBERG. Who opened the briefcase, me or you? Lulu, schmulu, let bygones be bygones, do me a turn. Kiss and make up. . .

LULU. You made use of me by cunning when my defences were down.

GOLDBERG. Who took them down?

LULU. . . . You taught me things a girl should't know before she's been married at least three times!

GOLDBERG. Now you're a jump ahead! What are you complaining about? (pp. 89–90)

We are not too far from the world of Max Miller's risqué stories, especially in the obviously meant *double-entendres* concerning taking down defences and being a jump ahead. The flippantly dismissive way in which the Jewish comedian Groucho Marx used to treat Margaret Dumont in the Marx Brothers' films may be remembered by way of comparison:

GROUCHO. One false move and I'm yours. I love you. I love you anyhow.

DUMONT. I don't think you'd love me if I were poor.

GROUCHO. I might but I'd keep my mouth shut.

DUMONT. I'll not stay here any longer and be insulted this way. . . . Will you keep your hands to yourself?

GROUCHO. Come on I'll play you one more game. Come on, the three of you.[27]

Another mask, which Goldberg seems to adopt more readily, is that of the expansive Jewish family man or business man. In this role, as in that of the cynical manipulator of women, there are a phoniness and an obvious humour which suggest Pinter is pushing the character towards the surreal:

> You know what? I've never lost a tooth. Not since the day I was born. Nothing's changed. . . . All my life I've said the same. Play up, play up, and play the game. Honour thy father and thy mother. All along the line. Follow the line, the line, McCann, and you can't go wrong. What do you think, I'm a self-made man? No! I sat where I was told to sit. I kept my eye on the ball. School? Don't talk to me about school. Top in all subjects. And for why? Because I'm telling you, I'm telling you, follow my line? Follow my mental? Learn by heart. Never write down a thing. And don't go too near the water.   (p. 87)

The rhetorical questions, the earnestly expressed clichés and the ludicrous non-sequiturs are characteristic of certain music-hall routines, but some of these features of the language also point to the confident conformist figure, the alien who has successfully integrated himself into English society. For him the phrase from Sir Henry Newbolt about playing the game, the earlier reference to Uncle Barney, 'respected by the whole community', and the comments on seeing 'how the MCC was getting on overseas' and having 'A little Austin, tea in Fullers, a library book from Boots' (pp. 37–8, 66) are all touchstones of, as it were, his credibility as a well-adjusted, cultivated English gentleman. When he adopts the mask of efficient bureaucratic organisation man his personality seems to undergo almost as appreciable a shift as his mode of delivery: 'The main issue is a singular issue and quite distinct from your previous work. Certain elements, however, might well approximate in points of procedure to some of your other activities' (p. 40). Even here, however, the comic element remains, as we see Goldberg in his role of partner in a kind of double act with the less eloquent and relaxed McCann:

I can assure you that the assignment will be carried out and the mission accomplished with no excessive aggravation to you or myself. Satisfied?

MCCANN. Sure. Thank you Nat.

Stanley, the artist *manqué*, reveals, particularly in his dialogue with Meg, the cynical, tired, apathetic and embittered side of the clown figure, reminiscent, as Peter Davison[28] and other critics have noted, of the Tony Hancock character, especially in its pathetic, humorous insistence on its own worth despite obvious appearances to the contrary:

I had a unique touch. Absolutely unique. They came up to me. They came up to me and said they were grateful. Champagne we had that night, the lot. (*Pause.*) My father nearly came down to hear me. Well I dropped him a card anyway. But I don't think he could make it. No, I – I lost the address, that was it. (*Pause.*) Yes. Lower Edmonton.   (pp. 32–3)

In both the character of Stanley Webber and the radio–TV character of Anthony Aloysius Hancock there is a tendency to switch roles. To Meg, Stanley can be as rudely brusque as the Hancock of the early radio series was with his landlady-*cum*-secretary, Miss Pugh; Stanley would denounce the quality of the food and drink served up for him ('tea like gravy') in a similar manner to Hancock ('at least her gravy used to move about'[29]). When on the defensive Stanley adopts a polite cliché-ridden chatty style, again not far at all from the nervous self-reassuring tones of Ray Galton and Alan Simpson's creation. The menacing figure of McCann Stanley attempts to cajole in most amusing fashion:

I know Ireland very well. I've many friends there. I love that country and I admire and trust its people. I trust them. They respect the truth and they have a sense of humour. I think their policemen are wonderful. I've been there. I've never seen such sunsets. What about coming out to have a drink with me? There's a pub down the road serves draught Guinness. Very difficult to get in these parts.   (p. 52)

One is reminded of Hancock's technique of ingratiating himself with the Nurse in the famous 'Blood Donor' TV programme (although, of course, this postdates *The Birthday Party*): 'Nursing? . . . It's a vocation nursing. I've always said that. One of the highest callings a woman can aspire to. . . . Dedicated. Three years training . . . .'[30] Just after this Hancock attempts to soothe his own nerves prior to his first blood donation; he is told the doctor is a Scot. 'He's a Scotsman? . . . They're marvellous doctors, the Scots. Like their engineers you know, first rate. It's the porridge, you know. Lead on, Macduff.'

Katharine Worth writes too of Pinter's 'not so good actors' – those who tend to be reserved, quieter and introvert rather than extrovert.[31] Yet these characters, those who tend to hide their personalities – the enigmatic, predominantly silent figures such as Ruth, Teddy, Aston and Kate – can also make powerful contributions to the linguistic battles fought in the plays. Although they may lack the verbal fluency and the role-playing techniques of Pinter's 'good actors' they are in effect manifestations of Pinter's belief in actions speaking louder than words. As John Russell Brown says, 'For Pinter, position, gesture and movement is rich in statement. By these essential means his characters can "speak" without knowing it themselves.'[32]

In their silence, Pinter characters often assert a positive strength. For Ruth and Kate there is an assurance and a detachment about their comparative silence; for Aston a dignified simplicity; for Teddy an indication of his callous indifference. When they do speak at some length, they do so simply and usually most effectively. Kate, for example, in *Old Times* is mainly taciturn and non-committal throughout; she is the enigmatic figure that Deeley and Anna in a sense fight over. Only at the end of the play is Kate given an opportunity by the playwright to speak at length (if one discounts the rather bland generalisations about living in the city and the country, halfway through Act II). The speech is of startling poetic and emotional significance and its effect is equivalent to the resolution of the play (pp. 71–3). In it Kate rejects both Anna and Deeley; in her own phrasing she has long since smeared them with the same dirt and has regarded them as dead so far as she is concerned. For Kate, the assiduous taker of baths, the image of dirt is indeed a powerful one. Deeley is reduced to weeping and Anna to a prolonged silence and the play ends with the three in sharp focus. Pinter has again achieved a moving, theatrical effect from the balancing of words and silence. Aston in *The Caretaker* achieves a similar emotional and powerful effect in his curtain speech at the end of Act II (see p. 53). Once again Pinter has allowed a previously quiet, non-loquacious character to give an extended piece of self-revelation. The monologue is rendered the more moving by its being in effect a successful attempt to recover articulacy. The original problem with Aston was talking too much for his own good; the harsh medical treatment to normalise his speech and behaviour patterns have rendered him quiet and generally non-communicative, and the speech, ostensibly to Davies, but in effect to the audience, is a manifestation of his ability to recover his verbal powers of expression. The effect on the audience might legitimately be compared to the poignant, dramatic effect that an actor playing a character with artificial legs might gain on portraying his first, faltering attempts at recovering the ability to walk (for example, Kenneth More's performance as Douglas Bader in *Reach for the Sky*, a popular British film of the mid fifties). Aston will never attempt to talk as he did previously, but he has set himself a newer, simpler goal – the building of the shed in the garden.

The two strongest characters in *The Homecoming* are, arguably, Teddy and Ruth, who do little talking, preferring their actions and their silences to denote their often cold and calculating attitude to situations. When they do speak at any length what they say is clinical and deliberate. Thus Teddy distances himself from the others as he sees his wife rejecting him in favour of other members of his family: 'You just move about. I can observe it. I can see what you do. It's the same as I do. But you're lost in it. You won't get me being ... I won't be lost in it' (p. 78). At first glance the speech may be indicative of no more than a rather peevish, ostrich-like character opting out of any responsibility, possibly in a cowardly way. There are, however, other options open to the actor. Peter Hall has spoken of Michael Craig's Teddy as the 'biggest bastard of the lot, as well as being the withdrawn intellectual . . . when he went at the end . . . he was leaving them with their deserts. He was leaving her with her deserts. And he was the worst of the lot.'[33]

As for Ruth, in the section in which Lenny quizzes Teddy on fundamental philosophical questions it is she, relatively silent, who is given the most significant speech. For the former 'model for the body' the simple basic level of communication on a physical level is of paramount importance; she is to prove her point when her erotic activity speaks louder than her hesitant rather stilted phrases:

You've forgotten something. Look at me. I ... move my leg. That's all it is. But I wear ... underwear ... which moves with me ... it ... captures your attention. Perhaps you misinterpret. The action is simple. It's a leg ... moving. My lips move. Why don't you restrict ... your observations to that? Perhaps the fact that they move is more significant ... than the words which come through them. You must bear that ... possibility ... in mind. (p. 69)

She draws attention to herself, obtains a silence, creates a tension, and in effect demonstrates an actor's power to 'capture' attention. It is as if the actress playing Ruth were speaking directly to the audience; she is laying bare not just the expectations of men and women towards each other, but also revealing something of the craft of self-exposure through words and movement that the actor practises in front of an audience.

In conclusion, I feel that the reverberant void that is conjured up by this much-quoted speech of Ruth's, this concern with the surface, with that which is observed, and the implicit denial of a final 'meaning' behind human behaviour is fundamental to Pinter and partly may explain his anxiety about Nigel Dennis's criticism concerning the hollowness of his plays and their being mere exercises for actors. Katharine Worth, in mentioning this anxiety of Pinter's, points most revealingly to a link between Pinter's art and life:

> Pinter went on to say in an interview with Mel Gussow, *New York Times Mag.*, Dec. 1971, that he was fascinated and troubled by this [Dennis's] account. I think one can see why. It's so near the truth: there is so much posturing, acting, mimicry, one does begin to wonder . . . if there's anything real behind. I think, though, that this worry is Pinter's too, and that one of the reasons why he is generally found so absorbing and haunting, as well as funny, is that he is touching an uneasiness his audience knows from their experience of themselves.[34]

This study uses Dennis's criticism as its point of departure. It attempts to show that there are indeed very strong connections between Pinter's work as an actor and his plays; but that these connections are creative ones relating to Pinter's distinctive vision of the world, not, as Dennis supposed, evidence of superficiality or triviality.

Appendix

PLAYS ACTED IN BY HAROLD PINTER, 1949–59

Year/date of first performance	Play	Type of play/author	Role played
AT CHESTERFIELD HIPPODROME FOR A SHORT SEASON			
1949–50	Dick Whittington and his Cat	Pantomime	Minor
WITH ANEW MCMASTER IN IRELAND			
1951–2 and late 1953	As You Like It	Shakespeare	Charles the Wrestler
	Hamlet	Shakespeare	Horatio
	King Lear	Shakespeare	Edgar/Edmund
	Macbeth	Shakespeare	Macduff
	Othello	Shakespeare	Cassio/Iago
	The Merchant of Venice	Shakespeare	Bassanio

Year/date of first performance	Play	Type of play/author	Role played
	The Taming of the Shrew	Shakespeare	Hortensio
	Oedipus	Sophocles	Creon
	An Ideal Husband	Wilde	Sir Robert Chiltern
	Lady Windermere's Fan	Wilde	Lord Windermere
	The Importance of Being Earnest	Wilde	John Worthing

WITH DONALD WOLFIT AT THE KING'S THEATRE, HAMMERSMITH

Year/date of first performance	Play	Type of play/author	Role played
Feb–April 1953	As You Like It	Shakespeare	Jaques de Boys
	King Lear	Shakespeare	Knight
	Macbeth	Shakespeare	Second Murderer
	Merchant of Venice	Shakespeare	Salanio
	The Taming of the Shrew	Shakespeare	Nicholas
	Twelfth Night	Shakespeare	Officer

Date		Type of play	Author	
	Oedipus the King (Oedipus Rex)/Oedipus in Exile (Oedipus at Colonus)		Sophocles	Elder/Countryman
	The Wandering Jew		T. Thurston	Duke of Normandy/Counsellor

WITH THE WHITBY SPA REPERTORY COMPANY

Date		Type of play	Author	
11 June 1954	Murder at the Vicarage	Whodunnit	A. Christie	Sophisticated artist
21 June	Here We Come Gathering	Farce	P. King and A. Armstrong	Major role

AT EASTBOURNE, AND THEN ON TOUR DURING AUGUST TO DUBLIN AND CARDIFF AND OTHER VENUES

26 July	A Horse! A Horse!	Comedy	L. du Garde Peach	Tops (minor role)

WITH THE HUDDERSFIELD REPERTORY COMPANY

15 Nov	Affairs of State	Comedy	L. Verneuil	Byron Winkler (US diplomat)

Year/date of first performance	Play	Author	Type of play	Role played
22 Nov	Late Love	R. Casey	Comedy	Young lover/amanuensis
29 Nov	Ten Little Niggers	A. Christie	Whodunnit	Major role
WITH THE COLCHESTER REPERTORY COMPANY				
28 Feb 1955	Point of Departure	J. Anouilh	Romance	Orpheus (romantic lead)
7 Mar	Waiting for Gillian	R. Millar/ N. Balchin	Thriller	Policeman
3 Apr	Down Came a Blackbird	P. Blackmore	Comedy	Egyptologist
18 Apr	The Uninvited Guest	M. H. Bell	Drama	Candy (title part, ex-mental patient)
2 May	Lovers' Meeting	C. Bond	Farce	Farce 'type'
9 May	The Wooden Dish	E. Morris	Drama	Minor role
16 May	Georgia Story	C. Cox	Drama	US slave-owner
30 May	Seagulls over Sorrento	H. Hastings	Comedy	'Villainous' Petty Officer

Date	Title	Genre	Author	Role
6 June	*No Escape*	Thriller	R. Davies	Minor role
13 June	*The Moon is Blue*	Comedy	F. H. Herbert	'Gentleman charmer'
[Spent summer in Ireland]				
26 Sep	*Reluctant Heroes*	Farce	C. Morris	Fierce PE Instructor
24 Oct	*The Living Room*	Drama	G. Greene	Psychologist
31 Oct	*You and Your Wife*	Comedy	D. Cannan	Husband (2nd lead)
7 Nov	*Serious Charge*	Melodrama	P. King	Minor role
14 Nov	*Witness for the Prosecution*	Thriller	A. Christie	Defending Counsel
28 Nov	*The Seven Year Itch*	Comedy	G. Axelrod	Psychiatrist
5 Dec	*Present Laughter*	Comedy	N. Coward	Minor role

WITH THE BARRY O'BRIEN COMPANY AT THE PALACE COURT, BOURNEMOUTH

Date	Title	Genre	Author	Role
5 Mar 1956	*Simon and Laura*	Comedy	A. Melville	TV producer
12 Mar	*Jane Eyre*	Romantic drama	C. Brontë/ D. Brandon	Rochester

Year/date of first performance	*Play*	*Type of play*	*Author*	*Role played*
26 Mar	*Rebecca*	Romantic drama	D. du Maurier	Mr de Winter
3 Apr	*Mad about Men*	Comedy	P. Blackmore	Lead
9 Apr	*Peril at End House*	Whodunnit	A. Christie	Hastings (ex-army)
16 Apr	*No News From Father*	Comedy	J. Huizinga	Family solicitor
30 Apr	*All For Mary*	Comedy	H. Brooke/ K. Bannerman	Comic lead
7 May	*Shadow of Doubt*	Thriller	N. King	MI5 man
21 May	*Lucky Strike*	Comedy	M. Brett	Industrial-relations expert
5 June	*The Whole Truth*	Thriller	P. Mackie	'Insidious' killer
9 June	*The Tender Trap*	Comedy	M. Shulman/ R. Smith	Lead (US husband)
18 June	*Way of a Wife*	Comedy	A. Merryn	'Erring' husband
25 June	*The Hollow*	Thriller	A. Christie	Minor role
2 July	*Bell, Book and Candle*	Comedy drama	J. Van Druten	Minor role

9 July	*Doctor Jo*	Drama	J. Morgan	GP (lead)
16 July	*Tabitha*	Comedy–thriller	A. Ridley/ M. C. Borer	Minor role
23 July	*Almost a Honey-moon*	Farce	W. Ellis	Comic lead
30 July	*Dead on Nine*	Thriller	J. Popplewell	Husky Canadian
6 Aug	*Off the Deep End*	Comedy	D. Driscoll	French mayor
13 Aug	*Love from a Stranger*	Thriller	F. Vosper/ A. Christie	Maniacal killer
20 Aug	*Ring for Catty*	Drama	P. Cargill/ J. Beale	Yorks miner
27 Aug	*A Woman's Place*	Comedy drama	W. Grimwood	Young airman
3 Sep	*Mr Kettle and Mrs Moon*	Comedy drama	J. B. Priestley	Bank-manager
10 Sep	*The Golden Earring*	Thriller	N. Waters	CID Inspector

Year/date of first performance	Play	Type of play	Author	Role played
WITH PHILIP BARRETT'S NEW MALVERN COMPANY AT THE PAVILION, TORQUAY, FOLLOWING BRIEF HONEYMOON WITH VIVIEN MERCHANT				
1 Oct	Bell, Book and Candle	Comedy drama	J. Van Druten	Black-magic author
8 Oct	Spider's Web	Whodunnit	A. Christie	Leading role
22 Oct	Ring for Catty	Comedy drama	P. Cargill/ J. Beale	Leading role
29 Oct	Separate Tables	Drama	T. Rattigan	Leading role
5 Nov	Mornings at Seven	Comedy	P. Osborn	(US) lead
12 Nov	Love from a Stranger	Thriller	A. Christie	Maniacal killer
19 Nov	Love on the Never-Never	Comedy	M. Rietman	Newly-wed
10 Dec	Mr Kettle and Mrs Moon	Comedy drama	J. B. Priestley	Minor role
30 Jan 1957	South Sea Bubble	Comedy	N. Coward	Minor role
11 Feb	A River Breeze	Comedy	R. Culver	Young lover
18 Feb	The Whole Truth	Thriller	P. Mackie	Detective Sergeant

Date	Play	Genre	Author	Role
25 Feb	*Gigi*	Romantic comedy	Colette/A. Loos	Lover
6 Mar	*Peril at End House*	Whodunnit	A. Christie	Leading role

[During the spring and summer of 1957 Pinter was on tour with *Doctor in the House*, a comedy-farce by T. Willis and R. Gordon, at Leicester, Cheltenham and other venues]

WITH THE ALEXANDRA REPERTORY COMPANY, AT THE ALEXANDRA THEATRE, BIRMINGHAM

Date	Play	Genre	Author	Role
19 July	*Hay Fever*	Comedy	N. Coward	Minor role
2 Aug	*Spider's Web*	Whodunnit	A. Christie	Inspector
2 Sep	*All My Sons*	Drama	A. Miller	Chris (young man)
30 Sep	*The Telescope*	Drama	R. C. Sherriff	Parson (lead)

WITH FRED TRIPP'S COMPANY AT THE INTIMATE THEATRE, PALMERS GREEN

Date	Play	Genre	Author	Role
26 Dec	*Worm's Eye View*	Comedy	R. F. Delderfield	Young schoolmaster
6 Jan 1958	*Subway in the Sky*	Thriller	I. Main	Plain-clothes detective
17 Mar	*The Vanity Case*	Whodunnit	J. Popplewell	Detective Constable

Year/date of first performance	*Play*	*Type of play*	*Author*	*Role played*
24 Mar	*Look back in Anger*	Drama	J. Osborne	Cliff

[In April Pinter understudied for N. F. Simpson's *A Resounding Tinkle* and *The Hole* at The Royal Court Theatre, London]

AT THE RICHMOND THEATRE, LONDON

29 Sep	*Any Other Business*	Drama	G. Ross/ C. Singer	Managing director

AT THE CONNAUGHT THEATRE, WORTHING

20 Oct	*Any Other Business*	Drama	G. Ross/ C. Singer	Managing director
27 Oct	*The Matchmaker*	Comedy	T. Wilder	Minor role

AT RICHMOND

17 Nov	*The Rocky Road*	Comedy	J. Carole	Estranged husband
9 Feb 1959	*The Stepmother*	Drama	W. Chethan-Strode	Disturbed young man
9 Mar	*The Hollow*	Thriller	A. Christie	Minor role

16 Mar	*A View from the Bridge*	Drama	A. Miller	Marco
25 May	*Out of Thin Air*	Comedy	D. Benfield	Amoral bachelor
24 Aug	*The Long and the Short and the Tall*	Drama	W. Hall	Corporal Johnstone

[Following this Pinter's acting-career became of secondary importance. On 19 Sep 1960 David Baron made his last appearance at Cheltenham as Goldberg in *The Birthday Party*. During the 1960s Pinter played three other roles of his own creation: Mick in *The Caretaker* at the Duchess Theatre (1960); Seeley in *A Night Out* on the BBC Third programme and in ABC's Armchair Theatre (1960); and Lennie in *The Homecoming* at Watford (1969).

Other roles on TV and in films include: Garcia in *In Camera* by J. P. Sartre (1964); minor roles in *The Servant* (1963) and *Accident* (1966), films directed by Joseph Losey; a solicitor in *Rogue Male* with Peter O'Toole (1978); an Irish dipsomaniac in *Langrishe Go Down*, directed by David Jones (1980).]

Notes

In the text, page references to Pinter's works are to the following editions, all published by Eyre Methuen, London.

Plays: One (1976), for *The Birthday Party*, *The Room*, *The Dumb Waiter*, *A Slight Ache* and the short story 'The Examination'.
Plays: Two (1977), for *The Caretaker*, *The Collection* and *The Lover*.
Plays: Three (1978), for *The Homecoming*, *Landscape* and *Silence*.
Old Times (1971).
No Man's Land (1975).
The Hothouse (1980).

In the references below and in the Bibliography, place of publication is London unless otherwise stated.

CHAPTER ONE: THE PLAYER'S PLAYWRIGHT

1. Harold Pinter, 'Writing for Myself', *Twentieth Century*, Feb 1961, p. 173.
2. Harold Pinter, 'Two People in a Room', *New Yorker*, 25 Feb 1967, p. 36.
3. 'An Interview with John Normington', in *A Casebook on Harold Pinter's 'The Homecoming'*, ed. John and Anthea Lahr (1974) p. 147.
4. 'An Interview with Paul Rogers', ibid., pp. 155, 153.
5. Bernard Levin, in the *Daily Mail*, 4 June 1965, p. 16; Clive James, in *the Observer*, 8 Oct 1978, p. 27.
6. Nigel Dennis, 'Pintermania', *New York Review of Books*, 17 Dec 1970, p. 22.
7. Harold Pinter, 'Writing for the Theatre', *Evergreen Review*, VIII (Aug–Sep 1964) p. 80.
8. Peter Brook, *The Empty Space* (1968) p. 73.
9. Harold Pinter, 'Pinter on Pinter', *Observer Review*, 5 Oct 1980, p. 25.
10. Information given in a letter from Richard O'Donoghue of RADA, 6 July 1978.
11. Pinter, in *the Observer Review*, 5 Oct 1980, p. 25.
12. Pinter, in *the New Yorker*, 25 Feb 1967, p. 35.
13. L. M. Bensky, 'Harold Pinter: An Interview' (first published in the *Paris Review*, 1966), repr. in *Twentieth Century Views: Pinter: A Collection of Critical Essays*, ed. A. Ganz (Englewood Cliffs, NJ, 1972) p. 29.
14. 'Harold Pinter Talks to Michael Dean', *Listener*, LXXXI (6 Mar 1969) p. 312; *Twentieth-Century Views: Pinter*, p. 21; *Observer Review*, 5 Oct 1980, p. 25.

CHAPTER TWO: APPRENTICE TO TWO MASTERS

1. Harold Pinter, *Mac* (Emanuel Wax for Pendragon Press, 1968) p. 16.
2. Ibid., p. 21.
3. Information from *Mac*, pp. 8, 10; and a personal letter from Barry Foster, a contemporary of Pinter's working for McMaster, 10 June 1980.
4. Pinter, *Mac*, p. 17.
5. Ibid., p. 18.
6. Ibid., pp. 5–6.
7. Ibid., p. 5.
8. Ibid., p. 8.
9. Ibid., p. 19.
10. Ibid., pp. 13–14.
11. Ibid., pp. 14, 9.
12. Ibid., p. 6.
13. Ronald Harwood, *Sir Donald Wolfit: His Life and Work in the Unfashionable Theatre* (1971) p. xiv.
14. Harold Pinter, 'The Knight Has Been Unruly: Memories of Sir Donald Wolfit', *Listener*, LXXIX (18 Apr 1968) p. 501.
15. Harwood, *Wolfit*, p. xii.
16. Ibid., pp. 178–9.
17. Ibid., p. 225.
18. Ibid., pp. 223–4.
19. Quoted ibid., p. 224.
20. Ibid., p. 223.
21. Ibid., pp. 41–2.

CHAPTER THREE: ENTER DAVID BARON

1. Arnold P. Hinchliffe, *The British Theatre 1950–70* (1974) p. 26.
2. R. C. Sherriff, *No Leading Lady* (1968) p. 57.
3. Terence Rattigan, *Preface to Collected Plays*, vol. II (1953) pp. xii, xiii.
4. Norman Marshall, 'The Repertory Theatres', *The Other Theatre* (1947) p. 192.
5. Ibid. (quoting St John Ervine), p. 192.
6. Richard Findlater, *The Unholy Trade* (1953) pp. 83–4.
7. Ibid., p. 84.
8. Ibid., p. 89.
9. Ronald Hayman, *The Set Up* (1973) p. 185.
10. Ibid., p. 186.
11. Leslie Smith, 'Pinter the Player', *Modern Drama*, Dec 1979, pp. 352–3.
12. *Acting in the Sixties*, ed. H. Barker (1970) p. 47.
13. Michael Billington, *The Modern Actor* (1973) pp. 173–6.
14. Pinter, in *Twentieth Century*, Feb 1961, pp. 172–3.
15. Pinter, in *Twentieth-Century Views: Pinter*, p. 20.
16. Ibid., p. 21.
17. Independent Television, interview with Melvyn Bragg, 22 Apr 1978.
18. Pinter, in *New Yorker*, 25 Feb 1967, p. 36.

19. Information from Kathleen Tynan, 'In Search of Harold Pinter', *Evening Standard*, 25 Apr 1968, p. 7; and Bragg interview.
20. Harold Pinter, 'New Year in the Midlands', *Poems and Prose 1949–1977* (1978) p. 1. The poem was written while Pinter was in a pantomime, *Dick Whittington and his Cat*, at the Hippodrome, Chesterfield, 1949–50.
21. Harold Pinter, 'The Drama in April', ibid., p. 14.
22. Harold Pinter, 'The Second Visit', ibid., p. 19.
23. Marshall Pugh, 'Trying to Pin Down Pinter', *Daily Mail*, 7 Mar 1964.
24. Tynan, in the *Evening Standard*, 25 Apr 1968.
25. Interview with the writer, 19 Sep 1983.
26. Pugh, in the *Daily Mail*, 7 Mar 1964.
27. *The Stage*, 29 July 1954, p. 28.
28. *The Stage*, 6 Sep 1956, p. 11.
29. Mrs E. Marsh, interviewed by the writer, 1 Aug 1980.
30. Findlater, *The Unholy Trade*, pp. 83–4.
31. *Bournemouth Daily Echo*, 13 Mar 1956, p. 10.
32. *Bournemouth Daily Echo*, 27 Mar 1956, p. 7; *Essex County Standard*, 4 Mar 1955, p. 8; *Bournemouth Daily Echo*, 28 Aug 1956, p. 10.
33. *Bournemouth Daily Echo*, 1 May 1956, p. 7; and 24 July 1956, p. 12.
34. *Whitby Gazette*, 18 June 1954, p. 6. Subsequent quotations from provincial newspapers are taken from the *Essex County Standard*, 7 Apr 1955, p. 8, and 17 June 1955, p. 8; *Torquay Herald Express*, 2 Oct 1956, p. 3; *Bournemouth Daily Echo*, 8 May 1956, p. 10, 11 Sep 1956, p. 7, and 5 June 1956, p. 6; *Torquay Herald Express*, 19 Feb 1957, p. 3; *Enfield Gazette and Observer*, 10 Jan 1958, p. 14; *Torquay Herald Express*, 13 Nov 1956, p. 3; and the *Essex County Standard*, 22 Apr 1955, p. 8.
35. Letter from Harold Pinter to the writer, 15 Dec 1981.
36. *Birmingham Weekly Post*, 6 Sep 1957, p. 6. The remaining quotations from provincial newspapers are taken from *Birmingham Weekly Post*, 4 Oct 1957, p. 6; *Enfield Gazette and Observer*, 3 Jan 1958, p. 14; *Richmond Herald*, 3 Oct 1958, p. 13, and 21 Nov 1958, p. 11; *Enfield Gazette and Observer*, 28 Mar 1958, p. 11.

CHAPTER FOUR: REP PLAYS AND PINTER PLAYS

1. Pinter, in *Twentieth Century*, Feb 1961, p. 173.
2. 'Harold Pinter Replies: Pinter Interviewed by Harry Thompson', *New Theatre Magazine*, XI, no. 2 (Jan 1961) p. 10.
3. Pinter, in *Twentieth Century Views: Pinter*, p. 33.
4. Ibid., p. 24.
5. Harold Pinter, 'Speech: Hamburg 1970', *Theatre Quarterly*, I, no. 3 (1971) p. 3.
6. Pinter, in *Evergreen Review*, VIII, p. 80.
7. P. Cargill and J. Beale, *Ring for Catty*, French's Acting Edition (1956) pp. 28–9.
8. Pinter, in *Evergreen Review*, VIII, p. 81.
9. Ibid., pp. 80–1.
10. John Elsom, *Post-War British Theatre* (1976; rev. edn 1979) p. 107.
11. Austin E. Quigley, *The Pinter Problem* (Princeton, NJ, 1975) pp. 148–9.
12. Ibid., p. 131.

13. Agatha Christie, *Witness for the Prosecution*, French's Acting Edition (1954) p. 71.
14. Pinter, in *New Theatre Magazine*, 11, no. 2, p. 10.
15. Martin Esslin, *The Peopled Wound: The Plays of Harold Pinter* (1970) p. 113.
16. Pinter, in *Evergreen Review*, VIII, p. 81.
17. Rosemary Casey, *Late Love*, French's Acting Edition (1954) pp. 47–8.
18. Pinter, in *Evergreen Review*, VIII, p. 80.
19. Ronald Hayman, *Contemporary Playwrights: Harold Pinter* (1970; rev. edn, 1974) p. 49.
20. Pinter, in *Twentieth-Century Views: Pinter*, p. 28.
21. Elsom, *Post-War British Theatre*, p. 107; and Billington, *The Modern Actor*, pp. 173–6.
22. *Enfield Gazette and Observer*, 21 Mar 1958, p. 11.
23. Pinter, in *Twentieth Century*, Feb 1961, p. 173.
24. *Casebook on 'The Homecoming'*, p. 12.
25. *Twentieth-Century Views: Pinter*, pp. 12–13.
26. Katharine J. Worth, *Revolutions in Modern English Drama* (1972) p. 90.
27. Quoted in Martin Esslin, *The Peopled Wound*, p. 34.
28. See Billington, *The Modern Actor*, p. 173.
29. See also Pinter, in *Twentieth-Century Views: Pinter*, p. 20.
30. *Bournemouth Daily Echo*, 8 May 1956, p. 10.
31. Dennis, in *New York Review of Books*, p. 22.
32. Pinter, in *Twentieth-Century Views: Pinter*, pp. 22–3.
33. Jan Kott, *Shakespeare our Contemporary* (1965) pp. 112–20.

CHAPTER FIVE: REVALUATION: PROPS, COSTUMES AND SETS

1. Pinter, in *Twentieth Century*, Feb 1961, p. 174.
2. G. B. Shaw, *Our Theatres in the Nineties*, vol. III (1948) p. 58.
3. Marshall, *The Other Theatre*, p. 192.
4. Ibid., pp. 192–3.
5. *The Wit of Noel Coward*, compiled by Dick Richards (1970) p. 15.
6. Pinter, *Mac*, p. 8; and Harwood, *Wolfit*, p. xii.
7. *Mac*, pp. 15, 9–10.
8. Ibid., p. 11.
9. *The Max Miller Blue Book*, compiled by Barry Took (1975) p. 72.
10. Ibid., p. 80.
11. Pinter, in *Evergreen Review*, VIII, p. 82.
12. Harwood, *Wolfit*, pp. 223–4.
13. Pinter, in *Twentieth-Century Views: Pinter*, pp. 27–8.
14. Smith, in *Modern Drama*, Dec 1979, pp. 8–9.
15. Ibid., p. 9.
16. Levin, in the *Daily Mail*, 4 June 1965.
17. Pinter, in *Twentieth-Century Views: Pinter*, pp. 27–8.
18. Ruby Cohn, 'The World of Harold Pinter', *Tulane Drama Review*, 6, no. 3 (1962); quoted in *Twentieth-Century Views: Pinter*, p. 80 (an early example).
19. Daphne du Maurier, *Rebecca*, French's Acting Edition (1939) pp. 87–90.
20. Ibid., pp. 33–4.

21. Pinter, in *Twentieth Century*, Feb 1961, p. 174.
22. Pinter, in *Twentieth-Century Views: Pinter*, p. 23.
23. Smith, in *Modern Drama*, Dec 1979, pp. 14–15.

CHAPTER SIX: REVALUATION: MOVEMENT AND DIALOGUE

1. Pinter, in *Twentieth-Century Views: Pinter*, pp. 22–3.
2. Pinter, in *Twentieth Century*, Feb 1961, p. 174.
3. John Russell Brówn, *Theatre Language* (1972) pp. 57, 59.
4. Harwood, *Wolfit*, pp. 223–4.
5. 'A Letter from Harold Pinter to Peter Wood, March 30, 1958', *Drama: Quarterly Theatre Review*, Winter 1981, pp. 4, 5.
6. Ibid., p. 5.
7. *Essex County Standard*, 22 Apr 1955, p. 8.
8. Peter Davison, *Contemporary Drama and the Popular Dramatic Tradition in England* (1982) p. 66.
9. 'Probing Pinter's Play', *Saturday Review* (New York) 8 Apr 1967, p. 58.
10. Dennis Welland, 'Some Post-War Experiments in Poetic Drama', in *Experimental Drama*, ed. W. A. Armstrong (1963) pp. 54–5; quoted in Hinchliffe, *Harold Pinter*, pp. 23–4.
11. Kenneth Tynan, *Show People: Profiles in Entertainment* (New York, 1979) p. 39.
12. *Casebook on 'The Homecoming'*, p. 148.
13. Ibid., p. 156.
14. Ibid., p. 145.
15. Ibid., p. 163.
16. Ibid., p. 160.
17. Pinter, in *Twentieth-Century Views: Pinter*, p. 20.
18. Kenneth Tynan, *Show People*, p. 30.
19. Pinter, in *Evergreen Review*, VIII, p. 82.
20. See esp. ibid., p. 82.
21. Oscar Wilde, *The Importance of Being Earnest*, Penguin edn (Harmondsworth, 1954) p. 301.
22. Peter Davison, 'Contemporary Drama and Popular Dramatic Forms', in *Aspects of Drama and the Theatre*, ed. R. N. Coe *et al.* (Sydney, 1965) p. 173.
23. Quigley, *The Pinter Problem*, p. 66.
24. Worth, *Revolutions in Modern English Drama*, p. 98.
25. *Casebook on 'The Homecoming'*, pp. 163–5.
26. Ibid., p. 163.
27. *Why a Duck?*, ed. Richard J. Anobile (1972) pp. 33–4. (The extract is from the film *Cocoanuts*.)
28. Davison, in *Aspects*, esp. pp. 152, 181–3.
29. 'Sunday Afternoon at Home', *Hancock's Half Hour*, BBC radio, 22 Apr 1958. Available on the Pye record *This is Hancock*.
30. 'The Blood Donor', *Hancock's Half Hour*, BBC TV, 1 Oct 1961. Available on the Hallmark record *The Best of Hancock*.
31. Worth, *Revolutions in Modern English Drama*, p. 98.
32. Brown, *Theatre Language*, p. 57.
33. *Casebook on 'The Homecoming'*, p. 20.
34. Worth, *Revolutions in Modern English Drama*, pp. 96–7.

Bibliography

PRIMARY SOURCES

The plays and other creative writings of Harold Pinter are published by Eyre Methuen. With the exception of *The Hothouse* (1980), all the plays written up to 1980 are included in four collections: *Plays: One* (1976), *Plays: Two* (1977), *Plays: Three* (1978) and *Plays: Four* (1981). These also include a few short stories and other prose pieces. *Other Places* (1983) includes Pinter's most recent plays (*A Kind of Alaska*, *Victoria Station*), and *Poems and Prose 1949–1977* (1978) collects his non-dramatic writing. The editions of Pinter's plays cited in the present study are listed on p. 138.

Most of the plays in which Pinter acted during his years in rep were published in French's Acting Editions. Details of the works quoted in the present study are given as appropriate in the Notes, where also details will be found of the reviews cited from provincial newspapers.

ARTICLES BY PINTER

'The Knight Has Been Unruly: Memories of Sir Donald Wolfit', *Listener*, LXXIX (18 Apr 1968) p. 501.
'A Letter from Harold Pinter to Peter Wood, March 30, 1958', *Drama: Quarterly Theatre Review*, Winter 1981, pp. 4–5.
Mac (Emanuel Wax for Pendragon Press, 1968); repr. in *Plays: Three* (1978).
'Memories of Cricket', *Daily Telegraph Magazine*, 16 May 1969, pp. 25–6; repr. in *Poems and Prose 1949–77* (1978) p. 89, as 'Hutton and the Past'.
'Pinter on Pinter', *Observer Review*, 5 Oct 1980, pp. 25, 27.
'Speech: Hamburg 1970', *Theatre Quarterly*, I, no. 3 (1971) pp. 3, 4; repr. in *Plays: Four* (1981).
'Writing for Myself', *Twentieth Century*, Feb 1961, pp. 172–5.
'Writing for the Theatre', *Evergreen Review*, VIII (Aug–Sep 1964) pp. 80–2.

INTERVIEWS WITH PINTER

'Filming *The Caretaker*: Harold Pinter and Clive Donner interviews by Kenneth Lavander', *Transatlantic Review*, 13 (Summer 1963) pp. 17–26.
Gussow, M., 'A Conversation with Harold Pinter', *New York Times Magazine*, 5 Dec 1971, pp. 42–3, 126–36.
L. M. Bensky, 'Harold Pinter: An Interview', originally published as 'The Art of the Theatre III', *Paris Review*, 39 (1966) pp. 13–37; repr. in *Twentieth-Century Views: Pinter: A Collection of Critical Essays*, ed. A. Ganz (Englewood Cliffs, NJ, 1972) pp. 19–33.

143

'Harold Pinter Replies: Pinter Interviewed by Harry Thompson', *New Theatre Magazine*, XI, no. 2 (Jan 1961) pp. 8–10.

'Harold Pinter Talks to Michael Dean', *Listener*, LXXXI (Mar 1969) p. 312.

'In an Empty Bandstand – Harold Pinter in Conversation with Joan Bakewell', *Listener*, LXXXII (Nov 1969) pp. 630–1.

'In Search of Harold Pinter: Interview with Kathleen Tynan', *Evening Standard*, 25 Apr 1968, p. 7, and 26 Apr 1968, p. 8.

'Trying to Pin Down Pinter: Interview with Marshall Pugh', *Daily Mail*, 7 Mar 1964.

'Two People in a Room', *New Yorker*, 25 Feb 1967, pp. 34–6.

ARTICLES CONCERNING PINTER

For publication details of *Twentieth-Century Views: Pinter* and *Casebook on 'The Homecoming'*, *see* Books section.

Billington, M., 'Our Theatre in the Sixties', in *Theatre 71*, ed. S. Morley (1971) pp. 208–33.

Boulton, J. T., 'Harold Pinter: *The Caretaker* and Other Plays', *Modern Drama*, VI, no. 2 (Sep 1963) pp. 131–40; repr. in *Twentieth-Century Views: Pinter*, pp. 93–104.

Cohn, R., 'The World of Harold Pinter', *Tulane Drama Review*, VI (Mar 1962) pp. 55–68; repr. in *Twentieth-Century Views: Pinter*, pp. 78–92.

Croyden, M., 'Pinter's Hideous Comedy', in *Casebook on 'The Homecoming'*, pp. 45–56.

Davison, P., 'Contemporary Drama and Popular Dramatic Forms', in *Aspects of Drama and the Theatre*, ed. R. N. Coe *et al.* (Sydney, 1965) pp. 143–97.

Dennis, N., 'Pintermania', *New York Review of Books*, 17 Dec 1970, pp. 21–2.

Dukore, B., 'A Woman's Place', *Quarterly Journal of Speech*, Oct 1966, pp. 237–41; repr. in *Casebook on 'The Homecoming'*, pp. 109–16.

Esslin, M., 'Godot and his Children', in *Experimental Drama*, ed. W. A. Armstrong (1963) pp. 128–46; repr. in *Modern British Dramatists*, ed. J. R. Brown (Englewood Cliffs, NJ, 1968) pp. 58–70.

——, '*The Homecoming*: an Interpretation', in *Casebook on 'The Homecoming'*, pp. 1–8.

Ganz, A., 'Mixing Memory and Desire: Pinter's Vision in *Landscape, Silence* and *Old Times*', in *Twentieth-Century Views: Pinter*, pp. 161–78.

Hall, P., 'Directing Pinter', *Theatre Quarterly*, IV, no. 16 (Nov 1974 – Jan 1975) pp. 4–17.

Hewes, H., 'Probing Pinter's Plays', *Saturday Review* (New York) 8 Apr 1967, pp. 56 ff.

James, C., review in the *Observer*, 8 Oct 1978, p. 27.

Lahr, J., 'An Actor's Approach: An Interview with John Normington', in *Casebook on 'The Homecoming'*, pp. 137–50.

——, 'An Actor's Approach: An Interview with Paul Rogers', in *Casebook on 'The Homecoming'*, pp. 151–73.

——, 'A Designer's Approach: An Interview with John Bury', in *Casebook on 'The Homecoming'*, pp. 27–35.

——, 'Pinter and Chekhov: The Bond of Naturalism', *Tulane Drama Review*, XIII, no. 2 (Winter 1968) pp. 137–45; repr. in *Twentieth-Century Views: Pinter*, pp. 60–71.

——, 'Pinter's Language', in *Casebook on 'The Homecoming'*, pp. 123–36.

——, 'Pinter the Spaceman', *Evergreen Review*, XII (June 1968) pp. 49–52, 87–90; repr. in *Casebook on 'The Homecoming'*, pp. 175–93.

Levin, B., 'No Happy Homecoming for Mr Pinter', *Daily Mail*, 4 June 1965, p. 16.

Milne, T., 'The Hidden Face of Violence', in *Modern British Dramatists*, ed. J. R. Brown (Englewood Cliffs, NJ, 1968) pp. 38–46.

Minogue, V., 'Taking Care of *The Caretaker*', *Twentieth Century*, Sep 1960, pp. 243–8; repr. in *Twentieth-Century Views: Pinter*, pp. 72–7.

Nightingale, B., 'Outboxed', *New Statesman*, 25 Sep 1970, pp. 394–5.

Pesta, J., 'Pinter's Usurpers', *Drama Survey*, VI, no. 1 (Spring–Summer 1967) pp. 54–63; repr. in *Twentieth-Century Views: Pinter*, pp. 123–35.

States, B., 'Pinter's *Homecoming*: The Shock of Non-Recognition', *Hudson Review*, XXL (Autumn 1968) pp. 474–86; repr. in *Twentieth-Century Views: Pinter*, pp. 147–60.

Storch, R. F., 'Harold Pinter's Happy Families', *Massachusetts Review*, Autumn 1967, pp. 703–12; repr. in *Twentieth-Century Views: Pinter*, pp. 136–46.

Taylor, J. R., 'Pinter's Game of Happy Families', in *Casebook on 'The Homecoming'*, pp. 57–65.

——, 'A Room and Some Views: Harold Pinter', in *Twentieth-Century Views: Pinter*, pp. 105–22.

Walker, Augusta, 'Why the Lady Does It', in *Casebook on 'The Homecoming'*, pp. 117–22.

Wardle, I., 'A Director's Approach: an Interview with Peter Hall', in *Casebook on 'The Homecoming'*, pp. 9–25.

——, 'Comedy of Menace', *Encore*, v (Sep–Oct 1958) pp. 28–33; repr. in the *Encore Reader*, ed. C. Marowitz, T. Milne and O. Hale (1965) pp. 86–91.

——, 'The Territorial Struggle' in *Casebook on 'The Homecoming'*, pp. 37–44.

Welland, D., 'Some Post-War Experiments in Poetic Drama', in *Experimental Drama*, ed. W. A. Armstrong (1963).

Wellwarth, G., 'Harold Pinter: The Comedy of Allusiveness', in *The Theater of Protest and Paradox* (New York, 1964) pp. 197–211.

Williams, R., 'Recent English Drama', in *The Pelican Guide to English Literature*, vol. VII: *The Modern Age*, ed. B. Ford (Harmondsworth; 1964) pp. 496–508.

RELEVANT BOOKS

Acting in the Sixties, ed. H. Barker (1970).

Anderson, M., *Anger and Detachment* (1976).

Anobile, R. J., *Why A Duck?* (1972).

Baker, W., and Tabachnik, S. E., *Harold Pinter* (Edinburgh, 1973).

Billington, M., *The Modern Actor* (1973).

Brook, P., *The Empty Space* (1968).

Brown, J. R., *Theatre Language* (1972).

Burkman, K., *The Dramatic World of Harold Pinter: Its Basis in Ritual* (Columbus, Ohio, 1971).

Burns, E., *Theatricality* (1972).

A Casebook on Harold Pinter's 'The Homecoming', ed. J. and A. Lahr (1974).

Cole, D., *The Theatrical Event* (Middletown, Conn., 1975).

Davison, P., *Contemporary Drama and the Popular Dramatic Tradition in England* (1982).
Dukore, B., *Harold Pinter* (1982).
Elsom, J., *Erotic Theatre* (New York, 1973).
——, *Post-War British Theatre* (1976; rev. edn, 1979).
Esslin, M., *An Anatomy of Drama* (1976).
——, *Pinter, A Study of his Plays* (1973), previously published as *The Peopled Wound: The Plays of Harold Pinter* (1970).
——, *The Theatre of the Absurd* (1974).
Findlater, R., *The Unholy Trade* (1952).
Gabbard, L. P., *The Dream Structure of Pinter's Plays* (Rutherford, NJ, 1976).
Gale, S. H., *Butter's Going Up* (Durham, NC, 1977).
Gascoigne, B., *Twentieth Century Drama* (1962).
Gielgud, J., *An Actor and his Time* (1979).
Hancock, F., and Nathan, D., *Hancock* (1969).
Harwood, R., *Sir Donald Wolfit: His Life and Work in the Unfashionable Theatre* (1971).
Hayman, R., *Harold Pinter* (1970).
——, *The Set Up* (1973).
Hinchliffe, A., *British Theatre 1950–70* (1974).
——, *Harold Pinter* (New York, 1967).
Kaller, J., *Actors on Acting* (New York, 1979).
Kennedy, A., *Six Dramatists in Search of a Language* (Cambridge, 1975).
Kerr, W., *Harold Pinter*, Columbia Essays – Modern Writers (New York, 1967).
Kitchin, L., *Drama in the Sixties: Form and Interpretation* (1966).
Kott, J., *Shakespeare our Contemporary* (1965).
Leech, C., *The Dramatist's Experience* (1970).
Marshall, N., *The Other Theatre* (1947).
The Max Miller Blue Book, compiled by B. Took (1975).
Ould, H., *The Art of the Play* (1948).
Quigley, A. E., *The Pinter Problem* (Princeton, NJ, 1975).
Rattigan, T., *Collected Plays*, vol. II (1953).
Roy, E., *British Drama since Shaw* (Carbondale, Ill., 1972).
Schroll, H. T., *Harold Pinter: A Study of His Reputation (1958–69)* (Metuchen, NJ, 1971).
Shaw, G. B., *Our Theatres in the Nineties* (1948).
Sherriff, R. C., *No Leading Lady* (1968).
Styan, J. L., *The Dark Comedy: The Development of Modern Tragic Comedy* (Cambridge, 1962).
——, *Drama, Stage and Audience* (1975).
Taylor, J. R., *Anger and After* (1969).
——, *The Rise and Fall of the Well-made Play* (1967).
Trewin, J. C., *Drama in Britain 1951–1964* (1965).
Trussler, S., *The Plays of Harold Pinter: An Assessment* (1973).
Twentieth-Century Views: Pinter: A Collection of Critical Essays, ed. A. Ganz (Englewood Cliffs, NJ, 1972).
Tynan, K., *Alec Guinness* (1961).
——, *Show People* (1980).
Wellwarth, G. E., *The Theater of Protest and Paradox* (New York, 1964).
The Wit of Noël Coward, ed. D. Richards (1970).
Worth, K., *Revolutions in Modern English Drama* (1972).

Index